The Handsome Man's Guide

To Being Handsome

By Kevin Shively

Copyright © 2011 by Kevin Shively

This book is a work of fiction, no matter how true the contents seem. It is intended for entertainment, and should be read as such. Facts and incidents may be skewed or fabricated, especially if you're an ex-girlfriend who is offended by them. Also, if you are an ex-girlfriend, or any other person, you should be aware that any resemblance to actual persons or events is coincidental.

All rights reserved. Permission must be obtained from the publisher prior to any reproduction or transmission of this work in any form or by any means – electronic or mechanical, including photocopying, recording or digital. Requests for permission should be addressed to Kevin Shively at Kevin@kevinsaysthings.com…I'll probably say yes.

LIBRARY OF CONGRESS CATALOGING-IN-PUBLICATION DATA

Shively, Kevin P.

The Handsome Man's Guide to Being Handsome

ISBN 978-1-105-24814-6

Content ID: 12114605

Contents

About The Author

Prologue – So You're a Handsome Man

Part One – Living the Lie

Part Two – Pretending You Care

Part Three – Loving Chicks That Love a Handsome Man

Part 4 – Relationships Are About Winning

Epilogue – A Handsome Man Would Have Learned Something

THANK YOU!

A huge thank you goes out to The Jedi Council (TiTTie...s). Alva, Chris, Joey, Sean, Reid and Derek, you guys pushed me when nothing was funny.

Thank you to my heterolifemate Tim Bowman, who started telling jokes with me over ten years ago and is still finding the funny in all the bullshit.

Thank you to my folks for dealing with the reaction that their extended families and friends may have to this book,

And to Shannon who dealt with more ex-girlfriend jokes than any girl should have to. You're amazing.

Thank you to the good folks at Dockers® for their support, both socially and with that sweet, sweet cash money. You guys are the best and your pants make me feel like a million bucks.

Finally, thank you to Stephen T. Colbert, aka "Papa Handsome Man" for the interview and subsequent *Colbert Bump* that I fully expect to receive once this book goes on sale. My people (aka "me on Twitter") will be in touch shortly.

About The Author

Kevin Shively is handsome.

- Prologue -

So You're a Handsome Man

I take it that since you're reading this book, you fancy yourself somewhat of a handsome man. Well good for you!

What...you want a cookie or something?

It's not like you're the first handsome man to walk this earth. George Clooney, Denzel Washington, Jesus, the dude from the Dockers commercials, David Beckham, me, my dad, Morris Chestnut, my grandpa, *his* grandpa, Neil Patrick Harris, Brad Pitt, Tom Brady, the baby from the e-trade commercials, Ben Affleck...all handsome men.

Handsomeness has been around as long as the world itself. This is a fact:

"And on the eighth day, God gave Adam a chiseled jaw and washboard abs. This would later turn out problematic when Abel inherited this trait and Cain developed his mother's love of carbs...but my bad y'all...no spoilers." – **Genesis: 21: 37½**

Are you humbled? Did I knock you off your high horse? I hope not...because that was a test.

You're a handsome man dammit! You *belong* on a high horse. You're better than everyone else. You're the general of this army we call "humanity". Are you ready for the responsibility that this charge comes with?

Some of you might be saying, "But Kevin, being good-looking isn't really a responsibility is it? It's just a superficial character trait!"

...Put this book down right now you peasant. If you thought that, you don't deserve the advice you'll find in the following pages. The rest of you can stay, but watch your step. You've seen my wrath, and you don't want this iron fist coming down on you.

OF COURSE being good-looking is a responsibility!

"With any great power comes great responsibility" – Uncle Ben (or someone else, depending on the copyright infringement laws surrounding movie quotes and how harsh Stan Lee is with offenders).

If you're a handsome man and don't consider your looks to be a "power" then you haven't been utilizing your gifts the way the great spirits intended...or maybe your good looks are just so engrained into your being that you never paid attention to the effect they have on the world around you. That I can understand, but allow me to enlighten you:

The Power of Being Handsome

1. People give you stuff (seriously, did you think you got our corner office with a view into the local NFL stadium because you're talented and work hard? Don't be silly. It came to you for the same reason the cute waitress brought you an extra plate of nachos).

2. You don't get in trouble for stuff (if you do, you need to learn to smile more...everyone loves a smile from a handsome man. It makes the ladies go weak in the knees and the fellas feel like they can face anything...they can't of course, unless they're another handsome man).

Okay I guess that's pretty much it. Those are the main powers of your handsomeness, but used correctly? You can accomplish anything.

The world's problems could all be solved if we simply focused our efforts on getting free stuff and avoiding trouble...

Of course, by "The world's problems could all be solved" I simply mean "You could TOTALLY get digits from that hot redhead at the bar"...And isn't that why we're all here anyway?

This power is yours to use as you will. I'm not your father. I'm more like your Yoda or Obi Wan than anything, but the point is that there are certain responsibilities that come with this power. My goal throughout this book is to help you learn those responsibilities and manage your power. Your metachlorian count is off the chart, but you're untrained in the Jedi ways...and I can offer the guidance and training you need to be more awesome.

What I hope to help you develop here are the tools necessary to handle your handsomeness. From everyday life and office etiquette to dating and relationships; by the end of this book, you should be well equipped to navigate these troubled waters of ugly people and successfully use your gifts as a handsome man.

Here and there, I'll also offer advice to the women in your life...because let's be honest; they don't appreciate you and your handsomeness enough. Ladies, my advice to you will almost always be "just touch it a little bit" because that's very versatile advice when dealing with your handsome man.

I hope you're ready for this, because like it or not, you're about to get a whole lot of truth and knowledge dropped right in your lap...which is okay because, as a handsome man, you should be wearing your Dockers flat-front khakis...which are stain-resistant.

Let's go for a ride.

Part I

Living the Lie

- Chapter One -

A Handsome Man Keeps it Classy

    I hate to start the book off on such a low note, but I come to you with a heavy heart. Sure, that heavy heart may be wrapped in a body gifted by the gods and hidden by a smile that would make Aphrodite place 2AM booty calls, but that's all a ruse...for this heart is still heavy.

    Recently, something was brought to my attention that we in the scientific community have long feared: Chivalry is all but dead.

    For years, there have been theories as to the cause of its demise: Some say men got lazy. Others believe women killed it...Personally? I'm not one for conjecture. I'll leave that to better men than myself. All that I know is that chivalry is like Steven Segal...it's hard to kill.

You see, as long as gentlemen like me exist, chivalry isn't dead. As long as champions of respect, honor and other sexy words like that are around, chivalry is too. And do you know what, my lost friends? I can help you join our team. Let me be your own personal Gordon Bombay of respect.

PS: Ladies, "Hard to Kill" is a Steven Segal movie title and "Gordon Bombay" was the hockey/life coach of the Mighty Ducks...I just wanted to make sure you knew and didn't feel left out...chivalrous of me? Yes.

A Gentleman's Guide to Being a Gentleman

1. **Open and hold doors:** This is the No. 1 most gentlemanly thing you can do. It's super sexy to ladies. In ancient times, men would hold doors for ladies because doors were really heavy to keep out vampires and dragons and stuff. Women simply *couldn't* open their own door. Over time, this evolved into a sign of respect and courtesy. Now, with the inventions of revolving doors, handicapped buttons and the doorstop, men have forgotten this time-honored tradition...but doors still exist. Next time you hold the door open for a woman, watch her knees buckle as she walks past. You're a suave mofo and she's impressed. Good work.
2. **Stand when a lady joins your table:** This is the best way to stand out. You'll either be the *only* dude at your table to stand, or everyone else will do that "half-stand" thing to awkwardly follow your lead. Either way, it makes you the alpha male, which is super awesome. I'm not sure where this one started, but it's respectful. No matter what you've learned from D-bags on MTV who wear fitted tank tops and pour bottle-service Grey Goose on the breasts of orange chicks in tube tops, **women still appreciate respect.** Oh, and also this gives you a better angle to look down her shirt.

3. **Know which fork to use:** This is a gentlemanly skill that you should probably learn. If you haven't already, then just watch the scene where Julia Roberts learns this from the concierge in Pretty Woman. Also focus on Richard Gere...that dude is a gentleman...you know other than the whole "hiring a hooker" thing.

4. **Offer a hand as she gets out of the car:** Women dig this. It's "take charge" but in a "sensitive" way. They associate this with Hollywood or British Royalty: you're *presenting* them. Also, have you ever been sitting in high heels and tried to stand up? That shit is ridiculously hard! What...no one else ever tried on their mom's shoes as a kid? Okay fine, it's just me then.

5. **Dress right:** Are your plaid boxers showing right now? Yes? Then get out of the 90s. But also, pull your pants up. If you're reading this, my guess is that you're too old for that. You should probably also buy yourself some Dockers flat-front khakis. The first step to being a gentleman is *feeling* like a gentleman...and trust me; these pants feel gentlemanly. The second step is looking good and 4-out-of-5 women say they lose their minds over a pair of Dockers...Let me ask you a question: what kind of pants do you think The Beatles were wearing when women would throw panties on stage? (please don't research this)

6. **Walk her to her door:** "But Kevin, what if I don't think I'm gonna get any?" Are you kidding me? That's the only reason you walk a girl to the door? How would you feel if a rogue robot attacked her as she was fumbling for her keys huh? Probably not very good. Here's another scenario for you: You walk her to the door. A robot attacks. You defend her with a judo chop and a punch to the robot's chest that knocks its power source out, incapacitating it on the spot. She jumps into your arms and screams "*My hero!*" And then you kiss her on the hand and say "goodnight"

...now she's left to sit alone in her claw-footed bathtub surrounded by candles, thinking about you and listening to Silk's

"Let me Lick You Up and Down"...you think you're gonna get a second date? You bet your ass you are.

I hope this has helped you realize the folly of your recent ways my friend.

Practice these simple steps, and within no time, you'll be a smooth, sexy gentleman much like me. This is the single-most important advice I can give to any handsome man. Well...other than being rich because that's awesome (when you get to the next chapter, you'll realize how awesome of a segue that was)

- Chapter Two -

The Handsome Man's Guide to Getting and/or Being Filthy Rich

I'm going to go out on a ledge here and say something super edgy: Being broke sucks…One of your first lessons of being a handsome man is to stop doing it.

Time to Make Some Money the Old Fashioned Way!

Question: Do you know the best way to get rich?

Answer: Be born with money.

Did you try that? Did it work? If not, you should probably try harder, but when you inevitably fail at that, you should try something new. And that's where I come in.

I remember when I was poor; like you. It was a sad time in my life. It was nothing like now...you know...when I'm ballin out of control.

Being poor stopped being cool a while ago. I'd say you're allowed a two-year hangover after college where being broke is still acceptable. People expect it. You can blame your lack of funds on the fact that you're "interning" or "still finding yourself" or something else equally as pseudo-existential.

But after that? You should probably sell out. Every handsome man sells out at some point, and I've gotta tell you, it's pretty sweet. It's like a drug. Once I sold out the first time, it totally made me want to sell out more.

The best advice I can give you (if you weren't born rich) is to just be super good-looking and charming. People will give you money. That's how I made my millions.

Unfortunately, you will not acquire this talent naturally like I did. Some of you will have to work for yours...and I don't mean "grind it out and get promoted" or anything that lame. I mean you'll have to *act* rich.

It's a well-documented fact that rich people like to support other rich people. It's been this way for years. So how do you become rich? You convince them *you already are*. Then you'll start getting the perks that only the uber-rich can enjoy.

How to Act Rich So Rich People Will Love You

1. Go to the symphony. I recently did this and it was pretty much all rich people. I can tell this because they were all wearing suits. And not poor people suits either. One dude *even had cufflinks*.

When you're at the symphony, it's important that you close your eyes during the songs. DO NOT FALL ASLEEP. It will be tempting to do so, especially during violin or oboe solos (I'm not even going to waste my breath on the French horn...NO ONE can stay awake during those parts). While your eyes are closed, you must gently move your hand in the same rhythm that the conductor does. You'll feel stupid, and you'll look stupid, but that's a big part of being rich and ballin out of control at the symphony. All the old dudes were doing it.

During intermission, order a Syrah from the bar. It will cost you roughly $273 but this is a small price to pay for your eventual wealth. This Syrah will let the other rich dudes know that you are rich, and since you're the only person in the audience under 65 and you look as good as you do, one of them will try to adopt you. Accept the offer. Then you'll be rich. I promise. Then you can get the Dockers flat front khakis and start pullin mad chicks bro.

2. Read the Wall Street Journal on the train. The Wall Street Journal is the most boring newspaper ever. That's why old rich white guys love it. Every time they get super-excited about all the piles of money they have at home, they pull out the Wall Street Journal to bore themselves back to reality. If you're reading it, they'll assume you are also trying to calm yourself down after thinking about the morning swim you took in your Scrooge McDuck style money-pool. Then they'll invite you out for tea. Rich people fucking LOVE tea. Drink it slowly...not because that's what rich people do or anything it's just that tea is really hot and I don't want you to burn yourself.

3. Start a charity. This one's huge. Have you ever met a poor person who has their own charity? No. Poor people are too busy trying to stay alive to care about feline leukemia or whatever the hell your charity will support and/or fight. You should come up with a really sad sob story about why you have this charity, but then when you're talking to a suspected rich person, you can add "but really it's just for tax purposes" with a sly wink. If you play this one right, this suspected rich person will write you a check for lots of dollars of American money. Then you can spend it on a sports car, because you need to get around and do your charitable stuff. Also, that car is now a tax write off, so really you're just legitimizing your claim.

4. Play Croquet. From what I can surmise (also, use words like "surmise"...they love that shit), croquet is like golf for really lazy people. Your ball is bigger, you don't have to hit it very far, you just gotta make it through a hoop instead of into a hole, and of course, you can keep your butler nearby.

5. Get a butler. Just hire one of your friends to pretend they're your butler when you invite your new rich friends over for croquet games. This way, you can look down on someone. If you didn't have a butler, you'd be the lowest form of life there, since everyone else is rich.

6. Talk about your "investment properties"...I'm pretty sure this is just a game that rich people play, because as far as I can tell, no property is an "investment" in this economy.

7. This is the most important thing I can tell you: Get yourself some Dockers Flat Front Khakis! Because (and pay attention because this is important) I figure if I keep talking about them, they might give me some money for mentioning them so much, and that would be a sweet way to get rich as well.

If there's one thing I've learned from rich people, it's that they don't care about other people, so you were stupid for reading this...unless you buy **Dockers Flat Front Khakis**...then you're awesome.

- Chapter Three -

The Handsome Man's Urban Survival Guide: It's Not Okay to Shoot the Hookers

I spent the last two years living in the suburbs and working in the even-more-suburby suburbs. It was bad. I was constantly waking up on Saturday mornings with a deep urge to prune Azalea bushes. The scary part is that I don't even know what the hell an Azalea is (best guess: some kind of cheese sandwich).

When you live in the suburbs, you forget that there's a whole magical world out there where the sound of a lawn mower is replaced by sirens and constant gunfire, and a place where the smell of barbecue is replaced by urine and fear. IT'S GREAT!

My office just moved into the International District (this is what liberal cities like Seattle call "Chinatown"), and I moved back downtown. There were a lot of things I'd forgotten about living in the city, so I did some homework: I watched every movie that takes place in an urban setting, I followed some dude with a guitar around until he saw me, and I listened to a bunch of rap music. Then I put together a survival guide. If you're a good-looking fella who's new to a major metropolitan area, you should pay close attention to this chapter, as it could save your life.

URBAN SURVIVAL GUIDE

- Chicks in the city love a dude in flat front pants. HAVE YOU SEEN THE DOCKERS COMMERCIALS?!?! Get some flat front khakis. *Then* you'll be ready to get the girls.

- You'll most likely befriend a black homeless man that lives near your building. DO NOT FEED HIM AFTER MIDNIGHT. Also, there's a good chance he will be a schizophrenic ex-fighter or cello player. You can get rich off this. Hang out with him, invite him into your home, and then write a movie or book about it. Just ask Josh Hartnett or Robert Downey Jr. Your new homeless friend should be named "Duke", but if he's not, you should give him a nickname and it's *very* important that you invent a high-five; this makes you tight. This is how homeless people solidify their bond.

- Your likelihood of being taken hostage by a hot female banker robber who falls in love with you and splits half the money she gets away with is higher. That never happens in the suburbs, but it's what I do for lunch on Tuesdays.

- The city is full of gangs. They're everywhere. Make sure to check in your closets and basements because there might be a gang hiding in there: Gangs love hideouts. If you encounter a gang in the wild, DO NOT PLAY DEAD. They're not bears you idiot. The best thing to do in this situation is mimic an old white lady. I just watched Kathy Bates in the new hit ABC show "Harry's Law" and trust me...gangs LOVE old white ladies.

- You'll probably meet a cute hipster girl in the Laundromat. Which is weird since buildings ALL have their own laundry rooms, but you'll probably go to one anyway because everyone loves folding their undies in public (yeah I fold my undies, so what?). When you meet this Laundromat vixen, make sure you have something clever to say like "Damn girl that American Apparel dress is *super* skinny, can I buy you a sandwich and make sex to your face?" She'll fall in love *immediately*.

- Before you go to a restaurant, learn everything you can about Jalisco, Mexico. I don't care if you're going to a restaurant called *Traditional Chinese Food Made by Real Chinese People*. **TRUST ME:** *Regardless* of the ethnic cuisine you are eating, everyone in the kitchen is from Jalisco, Mexico.

- Take the train. Not because it's easier to commute on the train or anything, but because there will be a lot of girls in pencil skirts on their way to work in the financial district and the pencil skirt is the greatest invention ever. This is an urban phenomenon. Girls from the suburbs wear pant suits, and not the sexy black polyester kind that makes them look confident and tall either...ugly brown ones.

> ***It's okay to approach the girl in the pencil skirt, just make sure you are doing it as the train is coming to a stop so you can "accidentally" fall into her lap...then when you're at the hospital getting her pelvis checked for hairline fractures, you guys can laugh and laugh about how ridiculous gender equality laws are.*

- And finally: You're safer in the city than in the suburbs. If you don't believe me, take this into consideration: Robocop doesn't go to the suburbs.

I hope this helps. In no time, you'll be smooth and confident and living an interesting urban life. Pretty soon you'll be stumbling home from the bars and paying a hooker to have sex in the back of a car before you shoot her in the face with a bazooka and take your money back...wait that might be Grand Theft Auto...Shit, I've gotta go apologize to some people.

- Chapter Four -

The Handsome Man's Guide to Decorating an Apartment...Handsomely

One of the hardest parts of being a grown-up handsome man is *accepting* that you're an adult now. You don't have someone to pick up your laundry, cook for you, tell you when to get up, or do your homework for you ....but enough about the girls across the hall in college.

Those times are over...unless you got married right away. The rest of us need to learn to survive on our own. It's a cold cruel world out there, and Snape killed Dumbledore so you're on your own.

But let me tell you something: It's gonna be alright. I'm here to be your Hermoine (creepy). I'm not your teacher, I'm your friend who will help guide you through these troubled waters and sometimes hold your hand for too long so that the red-headed guy I'm crushing on gets jealous...wait, where was I?

Right: now like any self-improvement process: you need to start in the home. Home is where the start is (hahaha...that was a delightful play-on-words that I added for you...you're welcome). You need to make sure your personal space is something classy...Something sexy...Something chicks will dig.

Home-Décor Checklist

Sit back and look around your apartment. Before we get into a shopping list, let's go over the things that are no longer allowed. You may need to rent a dumpster or storage unit if you have too many of these things still sitting around your place:

- "Fathead" stickers...no longer allowed.
- Neon beer signs or street signs...no longer allowed, unless they're hung next to your red felt pool table in a room with exposed brick.
- A "condom bowl"...okay come on, this wasn't even cool when you had it in college you sleazebag.
- A Redbull cooler...no longer allowed.
- A stack of Playboys in the bathroom...no longer allowed.
- A seven-foot bong with an NWA sticker on it as the centerpiece of your coffee table...no longer allowed.
- A framed photocopy of your MIP arrest mugshot...no longer allowed.
- A Nerf hoop...no longer allowed, except in your office. If you have a home office, this is acceptable.
- Cheap generic empty booze bottles lining your cabinet tops...I mean was that ever really cool? No longer allowed!

27

- Any and all furniture you owned in college...no longer allowed.

If you have a question about whether something you have should be on the list, then the answer is clearly "yes"...throw it out. You're starting fresh like John Leguizamo when he got rich in the movie "Empire"....also, *how legit* was Empire, huh? That movie was awesome!

Now that we've cleared out your entire house/apartment/condo, doesn't it feel better? We've got plenty of room to class your place up to a point where girls will want to come over and play scrabble with you.

There are several things you need to sexify your apartment. And let's be honest, the first step is probably "get a new apartment"...preferably with an exposed brick accent wall next to your floor-to-ceiling windows that look out on your respective city or body of water...if you can't afford a $2500/month rent payment, then there are other tricks. Here they are:

Decorating Tips to Start Living Sexy: Adult Style

1. **An area rug:** Nothing says "I'm aware of space and junk" like an area rug. Having hardwood floors was a good decision. I'm proud of you. But girls still like soft stuff. Get an area rug. Not bright colors. You're classy now remember? Budweiser red isn't a good look for you.
2. **An L-shaped couch that's leather on the bottom half and suede on the top:** This is the "mullet" of decorating. And by that I mean "it's awesome". Or I assume it is. When you walk through ikea, these make up 80% of their couch population so it's *gotta* be trendy. I don't know why I need leather on the part I don't sit on, but it looks sexy. Women *love* leather. If you don't believe me, ask her to show you her boot collection (don't do that, it's creepy).

3.   **A wine rack:** I don't care if you drink wine. You have to have one. Fill it with bottles of Two Buck Chuck and just flip em upside down so the labels don't show. This adds some sophistication that will mask the R&R Whiskey you have in the kitchen cabinet. The goal is for them to sit there long enough that they get dusty, that way you can say you've been saving them "until they're ready to be opened".

4.   **Framed Artsy Photographs:** The blacker and whiter the better (what?). You want to look all artsy and modern don't you? A picture of half of a tree root is a good one because it suggests that you're in touch with nature, grounded and also bold enough to like your photos cropped dangerously close (see what I did there? I turned bullshit into art. You need to learn how to do this).

5.   **Unframed Artsy Paintings:** Just some raw canvas with oil splashed across it. You don't even need an artist. The quicker you splatter some paint on the canvas, the better. If it looks like shit and makes people uncomfortable, then you've done what you're supposed to in the modern art world. Think Jackson Pollock but without the composition and talent.

6.   **A coffee table you didn't find on the side of the road:** No...an old cable-spool is NOT trendy and urban. It's ugly and it GAVE ME A SPLINTER RANDY! Sorry, I got off topic but that thing was stuck in my thumb for weeks. You need a real coffee table.

7.   **A coffee table book:** Your best bet here is something about architecture or nature. If that doesn't fit your personality, a cook book is fine. Personally, I have the "Lego" coffee table book...but you're not ready for that yet.

8.   **A pot rack:** Preferably one that you hang from the middle of your kitchen. People don't keep their pots and pans in cabinets anymore. You need to show them off. Hanging your pots and pans makes you seem like you've got your shit together. There's something about buying an accessory for your cooking accessories that does it for the ladies.

9. **A bed frame:** You can't get by with the mattress on the floor anymore. Oh, and I checked...the treefort bed set up they have in the ikea catalogue won't fly with classy broads.

10. **A mounted TV:** I have a nice TV, but I haven't mounted it yet, and I wish I had. It looks so much more grown-up! It's like "yeah, this is my house, I'll drill holes anywhere I want because I'm a grown up and my TV is too good to touch stuff."

11. **Some Dockers Flat Front Khakis draped across your fixed bed:** This makes it look like you're not trying, but also, a girl sees it and says "oh dag! He's rocking the Dockers Flat Front Khakis? This guy must have a good job because he's gotta look fly, but still has the leeway to dress semi-casual around the office!

You're ready. Go get that baller-ass pad so MTV can start filming your episode of Cribs...I'll bring the Bentley.

- Chapter Five -

The Handsome Nerd: This Ain't Your Father's Geek!

I'm kind of a nerd. You wouldn't guess it to look at me, but that's just because of my smooth vibe and the fact that I pull chicks like Bogart.

You wouldn't think, when looking at me standing here in a pair of Dockers Iron-Free Flat Front Khakis, that this sexy bastard just wrapped up a three hour argument about how a Vampire would ruin a dragon in a fight (and then explained to a friend why a Vampire-Ninja hybrid is the most deadly force the world has ever seen).

And I'm pretty happy about that. I don't want to be cool. Cool's not cool anymore. Nerd is. We live in a different generation. It's easier to be a nerd than it was for our parents. Athletes geek-out over video games on Twitter, rappers write songs about comic book characters. And yes, I hate to say it, but that douchebag football player that stuffed you in lockers in high school? He's probably building videogames at a studio that refuses to hire you.

It's true. Sorry old nerds. It's your fault for inventing video games. Before that, we never would have dreamed about coming into your world. Cool's gone underground. Everyone wants to be a nerd now.

This was made clear to me last night; I was talking with some friends about which movies Hollywood will probably remake next, destroying our childhood memories (we may have been a little dramatic about this), and no one brought up a movie about being a nerd and overcoming adversity after getting beat up and picked on for 3/4 of the movie…Let's be honest; that was Hollywood's bread and butter in the 80s.

- My buddy Ryan said **"The Warriors"** and I can totally see it, but instead of a rumble, it's now a dance battle…and instead of underground street gangs, they're all competing for a spot on BET's new dance show. Ryan cried for a minute when I said this.
- Patrick said **"Footloose"** and I have no question they'll remake this. It'll probably be in the Afghanistan, and instead of a pastor who's afraid of losing his kids to alcohol and this crazy outsider from the city, it's a Taliban War Lord who's terrified of this Western Devil who suggested his daughter show her nose when she dances with a same-sex partner *(Footloose has been remade since I first wrote this chapter, but I like my version better than the "Step Up" remake they actually came out with, so I'm keeping this one)*.
- Tim said **"Point Break"**, and none of us wanted to play this game anymore…

But do you know what wasn't mentioned?

"Revenge of the Nerds" or "Weird Science"

Revenge of the Nerds could never be remade. You know why? Because that's not how nerdiness works now. You don't have the "nerd group" and the "jock group". Have you seen The Social Network? JUSTIN TIMBERLAKE INVENTED NAPSTER! He's not a nerd. He sang the most gangster song ever: "Cry Me a River".

The old adage of "just wait til you're a grown up, because the nerds will be the rich ones and the jocks will be working in a garage somewhere" doesn't fly in this millennium.

Sure, Microsoft still has plenty of OG nerds working there...but they eat lunch with guys who played college football and nailed cheerleaders. The world is smaller and technology isn't that scary anymore. The meek aren't inheriting anything these days...sorry, guys who write the Bible.

The upside of this? Your "Weird Science" characters aren't inventing computer women, because nerds get chicks now. Have you seen *The Big Bang Theory?* I know me neither...I don't think anyone has.

The world's moving too fast these days, and the only people who can keep up are the people with jetpacks (and black people, but only because of the extra ligament in their legs).

If you don't like this change, you can blame James Vanderbeek. Dawson's Creek taught kids it was "cool" to speak eloquently, and things spiraled out of control from there. AC Slater is rolling over in his grave (Wait...I'm being told he's not dead yet).

So embrace it, America. We're a nation of nerds who also play outside. If you're just one of the above, you're slippin. A handsome man needs both sides of the coin.

Alright, I'll see you guys in the next chapter...I gotta go play Call of Duty on my Android at the batting cages.

- Chapter Six -

The Handsome Man's Guide to Being All Sensitive and Shit

I was on Twitter recently doing some Twittering, and I was told that I'm not sensitive enough. Fair criticism. I write a blog that makes fun of everyone. But then later that night, someone else told me that I'm *too* sensitive and I should "start writing about pottery and nail polish" because my manhood was suspect.

This has led me to the undeniable conclusion that these two statements cancel each other out and make me the PERFECT amount of sensitive. That was a "double-negative", which was a math reference for my Asian friends. You're welcome guys.

I'm a modern man. I drink tea with my grandma while darning socks out of kittens and "crying just to cry"...but then I go out in the mountains on ATVs with my Copenhagen-chewing buddies and we shoot those kittens with paintball guns just to hear them scream.

My point is this: The modern man needs to maintain a delicate balance between "sensitivity" and "masculinity" otherwise he'll never make it in this world. Fellas, here's your guide to making it in this world.

HOW TO BE HARDCORE SENSITIVE

- **Don't Watch So Many Male-Dominated Action Flicks:** Seriously guys, how many times can you watch *Predator 2* anyway? Danny Glover isn't THAT exciting. Instead, pepper in some sweet, sweet romantic comedies. I'd recommend *Speed*. Sandra Bullock and Keanu Reeves' love is hard to put into words. These two crazy kids are on a wild ride and bump into some colorful characters as they slowly realize that the foundation for a solid relationship is indeed sex. Oh, and I was just kidding about *Predator 2*, it's awesome...Also, shoot the hostage.
- **Get yourself a pair of Dockers Flat Front Khakis:** These pants are the manliest thing you can wear (Robert Redford has a bunch of pairs...probably), but they're also super soft and comfy (it'll be like a carebear is delicately cradling your genitals...but only if the carebears are over 18...Actually I'm gonna have to get back to you on that one, I don't need any lawsuits).
- **Buy Katy Perry's CD:** This is good advice because girls will think you have the same musical taste and that you're in touch enough with your feminine side to listen to "Firework" without feeling like less of a man. But also, I was looking at the CD jacket the other day and it's just a bunch of pictures of her with whipped cream on her naughty bits...And that's neat.

- **Eat More Frozen Yogurt:** its okay. You don't have to pretend that you're too cool for "Berry Bonanza Blast" covered in delightful fat-free strawberry syrup anymore. Fro-Yo is delicious and it's time you let the world know. Just make sure you throw a bunch of Heath Bar Bits on top of it. Heath Bar is delicious and chocolaty, but it's called a "Heath" bar which is the most masculine name for a candy bar ever.

Little known fact: the least manly candy bar is "Payday" which goes against intuition, but it was invented to distract women from the fact that they make less money. If you give them some chocolate along with their lower wages, they'll shut up long enough for you to sneak out of the building and get out on your yacht for the weekend.

- **Open Up Emotionally:** Haha, no I'm kidding. You can pretend on this one. Just watch *When Harry Met Sally* and learn to quote what Billy Crystal says.
- **Touch Her Shoulder:** Sound creepy? That's because you're not an emotionally volatile girl. You didn't just get into a huge fight with your mother and you're not feeling insecure at work right now. These girls love it when they're telling you about their problems (first of all, they love telling you about their problems) and you touch them understandingly on the shoulder. Just make sure you don't become the "creepy massage guy" of your office. No one likes that guy so stop doing it Bill, my shoulders aren't *always* tense!
- **Snuggle:** This is a dangerous path, but if you're up to the challenge, you should give it a shot. Snuggling is pretty legit once you get into it. It's super soft and cozy if she moisturizes, but it's easy to get carried away and then you wind up being the clingy one in the relationship who's constantly asking "what she's thinkin bout" instead of the other way around and all of a sudden she's the one who says "sandwiches" and actually as I'm typing this I'm thinking of ways to manipulate the system so this can happen because then we could take turns making sandwiches at

2AM and that would be awesome...I don't know if it can be done but I'll give it a shot next time some girl tricks me into dating her.

Well, at any rate: Make sure you're the big spoon to keep the dominance in the snuggling process.

I hope you've learned how to be more sensitive, but still be a badass. That's what I do and so far it's worked out pretty well for me. You should be like me so ladies will snuggle with you while you eat a sandwich and watch Speed.

- Chapter Seven -

The Handsome Man's Guide to Dinner Parties

Last night I became a man. Now look...don't jump to conclusions; I don't mean I had sex for the first time or celebrated my bar mitzvah or killed my first buffalo. Nothing that immature.

Last night I went to a grown up dinner party.

Before you get all high and mighty and say something like "Come on Kevin, my friends have dinner parties all the time!" you should know that I don't mean "we ate food at the same table and someone brought beer." I mean I went to a *dinner party*. This dinner party was on a houseboat. And I'm pretty sure it was the one from "Sleepless in Seattle."

To help further break down how much of a grownup I am now, I should tell you this: I brought wine. EVERYONE brought wine. The difference is that my wine didn't have a cool back-story from when I bought it on a backpacking trip through the Chilean mountains. Also, I didn't bring skinny bread (Apparently at a grown-up party you're supposed to bring this skinny bread called a "baguette" which is French for "this bread is stupid and rock hard but if we had two of them we could totally swordfight").

Are you impressed yet? Because I haven't even gotten to the guest list. I was THE ONLY person in the group who didn't have either a masters or a doctorate. Wait -- scratch that -- one Italian guy was still finishing his thesis because he's from Milan and I'd imagine that when you live in Milan, you're too busy having sex with supermodels and racing Enzos to have time for school.

Employers for these grownups included the Gates Foundation, Fred Hutchinson Cancer Research Center, Harvard (yeah...he WORKED there...but he also went there), some tech firm that probably works with NASA...and one girl had her own private practice...I don't even know what that means but it sounds serious.

Meanwhile, I write a blog about how girls have cooties.

I was *totally* John Cusack in High Fidelity. And in the midst of our Italian dinner cooked by a real Italian, I realized that being a grown up is *hard*. You have to care about stuff other than whether or not they'll bring back the TV show "Firefly" or whether or not the girl across the table's boobies are real or fake.

I know the majority of you are at a similar crossroad, so I wanted to put together some tips based on mistakes I made...As a handsome man, you'll be invited to a lot of grown up dinner parties, and these should help you pretend you're a grown up.

Oh, and I PROMISE...no boobie jokes for the rest of this chapter...

How to be more grown up than real grownups: Dinner Party Edition

- When someone invites you over for dinner, bring skinny bread. This is what adults do. Skinny bread and wine. If you want to *really* seem like a grown up, bring some kind of cheese you've never heard of. There's a good chance your host will already know about this cheese varietal, but its okay because you can just say "yes, this is my favorite gruyere. It really goes with the Chilean wine I brought."
- For God's sake, get yourself some flat front Dockers!
- Cloth napkins: All grownups have cloth napkins. I think they sell these at Pier One. The cloth napkin is important because it can match your table cloth, and grownups love when shit matches. Also, you should get more table cloths.
- Conversation topics should always revolve around current events, and you should have strong opinions that aren't really that ground breaking. Say things like "I think what Mubarak did to Egypt was awful. Just AWFUL!" This will cause people to agree with you and continue the conversation. You can just sit back and nod smugly because you were the catalyst for this grown up conversation. If you have a hard time paying attention, just picture boobies bouncing up and down and you'll automatically look like you're nodding in agreement (okay last boobie joke, I promise fo realz this time). Other acceptable conversation topics are: 401ks, the stock market, health care, and capitalism. Avoid comic strip references unless they're from the *New Yorker*.
- Eat your vegetables. Adults ALL pretend to like their vegetables. This is part of the game (this is the only game adults play, and there's no winner because everyone is eating vegetables).

- Talk about your mental health. Grownups love to share things that their "councilor" recommended to them. Councilors are a big part of being a grown up because they mean you're in touch with your flaws. Personally I have to make things up when we talk about this, because I have no flaws.
- No food fights. And if someone spills their wine, slurping it up or using a piece of skinny bread as a sponge are both also frowned upon.
- Call things "frowned upon"...Other words grownups use a lot are "activities" "ajar" and "agenda" (these are just the "A's", for a full list of grown up words, consult a real grown up).

Editor's Note: This last one is the most important of all. They say that those who don't learn from history are doomed to repeat it...Don't repeat my history.

- Under *NO CIRCUMSTANCES* is it okay to get drunk on wine, give a toast to your date's boobies and then climb up on the roof of the house boat naked planning to jump off, only to fall onto the deck because it's been snowing and it's icy and while you're laying there and the host comes up to check on you, you start laughing and yelling "I'm gonna live forever!" before you slap her on the ass making it awkward for everyone and you're asked to leave. This is a bad idea and is considered one of the worst breaches of dinner party etiquette...right after ritual sacrifice and suggesting an orgy to the cat.

You're now equipped to handle any dinner party another "adult" may invite you to. Oh, and "boobies".

- *Chapter Eight* -

Drinking Handsomely: A Party Guide

Have you upped your partying since college? You should have.

You're Thinking: *Yeah! Good call Kevin! My name is Sean and I like to party! Let's RAGE!*

Calm down Hank Moody. I'm not saying you should be partying *more*. I'm saying you should be partying *better*. There are certain levels to partying. You can jump around occasionally, but you should mostly stick to your particular genre...it's for your own protection.

Now you're thinking: "Kevin, why have you called me *Sean* AND *Hank Moody*? My name is CLEARLY Stephen!"

And to that I say: "Shut up Stephanie, obviously Sean likes to party and Hank Moody is a fictional icon so you should just be grateful that you were put in such great company."

But you might *also* be thinking: "What is my *Party Genre* Kevin?"

Now you're back on track. The whole "wrong name" thing was distracting, don't do it again...But I *can* help you with your Party Genre (PG).

You see, when you were younger, it was easy to party. For every high school, there's only one party. Tommy's parents are out of town and so that's where you party. You probably had three Mikes Hard Lemonades and decided it was a good idea to jump off the roof...you know...to impress Tiffany Swanson. But it *didn't* impress her and she went home with the stupid captain of the football team Jason Harrison and your ankle hurt for weeks and people called you "Fallout Boy" for the next year of your stupid so-called life and you got all emo and hated your parents for a while...but maybe that's just me.

And yes, I GET that chronologically, the nickname choice of that story doesn't make sense and none of those people are real. But I was trying to prove a point you guys: High school parties are all the same (except in the movie "Never Back Down"...that party was wicked awesome like an MTV show, but the old-school GOOD MTV shows). That's not how it is now. You have options. You get to decide which parties you enjoy.

I've put together a little manual. It's my hope for you that you will use this as a Yoda-like guide to help you ease your way into the correct social setting where, as a handsome man, you can enjoy the finer things life has to offer...like PBR and boobies.

Discovering Your Party Genre and How to Exist Peacefully With Other Genres

College House Party

Description: Let's get hammered! You don't have to think a lot in college. You don't even have to talk. The shitty music is too loud. You just show up, drink your weight in Goldschlager, do a keg stand, yell "WOOOOOOO" and sing a Journey song with a house full of people doing the same thing. You're allowed to break things, have sex in other people's beds with people you don't know, dance like a hooker and make out in public and/or streak. No judgment. This is the only party genre where this is allowed.

Attire: An ironic t-shirt and ripped jeans.

How to hit on chicks: Play a guitar. College chicks *love* the guitar guy. You know one chord, and she's too stupid to notice. Learn "Hotel California" or "More than words"...or whatever, they don't really care.

What to bring: Bring your own red cup. This way it looks like you paid to drink from their keg. This is the cheapest way to go about life in general.

EDITOR'S NOTE: I almost didn't include this one, but it's important to the framework. A wise man once told me "you have to know where you came from, to know where you are going". Also, I wanted to make fun of the douche with the guitar. You know who you are...Kyle.

Adult House Party

Description: This has *significantly* changed since the college party. At this house party, there's probably food, nice furniture, at least one pair of Dockers Flat Front Khaki pants (can you tell they helped pay for this book?) and the probability of a guitar guy has diminished by at least 27%. Also, there usually isn't dancing – wait…I misspoke. There usually isn't dancing *like a hooker*. Adults dance, but no touching unless it's a slow song or you're doing a twirly thing. Watch a Homecoming episode of "Saved By The Bell" and you'll know what to do.

The rules for a grownup house party can be conveyed much like those of Gremlins:

1. Stay away from the cheese dip

2. No keg stands before midnight

3. Compliment the host on their recessed lighting (grownups love recessed lighting…it has to do with something called "Ikea" but I don't know what that is).

Attire: Dockers Flat Front Khakis…Or their Chinos, which are delightful as well.

How to hit on chicks: Talk about how the current economic climate has swayed your decision to buy/not buy a house while some hot little philly is nearby. This will get her to think you're rich and/or smart. Then, when you first approach her, say or do something hysterical (you gotta come up with this on the fly, bro…I can't do all your work for you). This will get her to think you have everything. Seal the deal by asking her to go camping (j/k, don't do that!).

What to bring: This isn't a dinner party. You still bring beer or a bottle of hard alcohol. The people who bring wine are usually too old or lame for this house party. They belong at the next type:

Dinner Party

Description: See "The Handsome Man's Guide to Dinner Parties"

Attire: Still Dockers Flat Front Khakis (they're so versatile!)

How to hit on chicks: You should have a date at the dinner party. If you don't, it's the host's plan to set you up with the one other single person there. If you're both guys? You're gay now. They just decided it for you.

What to bring: Wine and skinny bread.

Holiday Party

Description: If your holiday party has a theme like "Ugly Christmas Sweaters", you should immediately stand up, leave and go to a different holiday party. These are about as cool as Murder Mystery Dinners, but you don't get dinner and there's no murder (which are two of the three key elements to a good party). Holiday parties usually involve looking semi-swanky and/or slutty (i.e. New Years, Halloween, Easter Brunch etc.). Guys, you should wear a tie. You know what ties go great with? Dockers Flat Front Khakis (available at Nordstrom).

Attire: A Dockers "No Iron" button down with Flat Front Khakis...from Dockers (ladies, you can wear a slutty cocktail dress).

How to hit on chicks: Learn a very Holiday-Specific cocktail mixture and practice at home. Then, ask a random breezy (yeah I can say breezy, I have black friends) if you can make her a drink. She'll melt in your mouth (eww).

What to bring: The necessary alcohol or mixer to make your drink. ***Warning: no "cinnamon stick shavings"...unless you're hittin on a gay dude or Martha Stewart, then I'll allow it.

Adult Birthday Party

Description: This probably takes place in a rented out "VIP" room at a club or bar. The sad part about an adult birthday party is that if it's a dude, he probably had to spring for the room himself. And that makes you a bad friend. Be better. Your job is to get this friend so drunk they forget how old they are. That's not hard. Everyone there will buy them a shot.

Attire: A black button down that may or may not have tribal or tattoo looking designs on it. Girls, you're gonna bring back that little black cocktail dress (you know what? Let's just make that the standard because you guys look good in those things).

How to hit on chicks: Tell her about how tight you and the birthday boy are. It'll be loud, so you can do that creepy lean-in-and-touch-the-small-of-her-back-while-you-go-"what's that?" move.

What to bring: Cash for tequila shots. Presents aren't necessary.

Barbecue

Description: This is my personal favorite genre. Cookin' some meat. Sitting on a balcony or backyard patio chair, drinking a Corona and chilling with friends, playing dominos and a Sam Cooke CD. Plus, two words: Bocce Ball. If you don't play bocce ball then you and I can't be friends. BBQs are also good because they can start at noon. None of the other parties on this list allow you to party all day. That's why I win.

Attire: Whatever you want dude. BBQs don't judge!

How to hit on chicks: Slowly! You've got ALL DAY. Just set the frame work for the inevitable eye-lock across the fire pit that night that says "look I'm pretty drunk, but I thought you were cool four hours ago when I was sober too'"

What to bring: Some chicken wings or burger buns and a case of your favorite summer time brew.

Office Christmas Party

Description: Ahhhh the office Christmas party...Setting for "mistakes that make staff meetings awkward" since 1823. Everyone loves the office Christmas party. Let's all blow off some steam together! Plus, Stephanie has never gotten as skanked up as she did for the office Christmas party, am I right fellas? Huh? Also, there's usually an open bar, which is neat.

Attire: Semi-formal. Which is best exemplified by the Dockers Flat Front Khaki Pant.

How to hit on chicks: You don't have to. Sheila in accounting knows who's been checkin' you out. She's gonna make sure Lisa from Marketing gets lubed up (with alcohol perve) to come make her move on *you*.

What to bring: Enough cash for a hotel room because you won't be okay to drive, and Lisa isn't tired. She wants to "watch a movie" tonight.

So there you have it. Hopefully this chapter helps you find out what kind of adult handsome gentleman you are. And hopefully it's an awesome one...an awesome one who wears Dockers Flat Front Khaki Pants.

- Chapter Nine -

The Handsome Man's Guide to the Bar Scene

Have you ever *accidentally* wound up in a club? It's awful. You're tagging along with your friends, possibly chatting up Steven's cousin Kelly who's in from out of town, you hand your ID to a doorman without paying attention to where you are because Kelly's hair smells like roses after the first rain of spring and it's really distracting...and all of a sudden BAM! You're hit in the face with shitty techno, Axe Body Spray, sweat, glitter and shame.

At this point you immediately do one of three things:

1. If you're under 25 you unconsciously say to yourself "Okay fine let's get wasted because that's the only way I'll be able to deal with this hellhole."

2. If you're over 25 you turn into Danny Glover and just repeat all night "I'm getting to old for this shit"

3. If you're Asian you shout "Party rockers in the HOUUUUUUSE tonight!" and then you buy more shots of Grey Goose with pineapple backs because for some reason you guys LOVE clubs.

But I can't handle them anymore. It's been a while since I've been to one, but I got tricked recently (by "tricked" I just mean a cute girl said "Let's go to a club"). It was awful. Although...there is ONE awesome thing about clubs:

THAT WAS A TRICK! There's nothing awesome about $12 drinks after paying a $10 cover to get bumped into by glitter-covered girls that smell like Herpes as they try to decide which new d-bag they'll sleep with and then yell at for "tricking them into bed" in the morning.

You're a grown-up now guys. I'm not telling you to stay out of bars/clubs. Do what you want to do. That's part of being a grown-up too. I don't even have a bed time anymore. It's great! But there are certain habits and attitudes that a grown-ass man should adhere to when out enjoying his city's nightlife.

The Bar Scene: A Handsome Man Guide

Pressed Shirts: I generally adhere to a rule that if you dress up MORE to go out to a bar than you do to go to work; you're doing something terribly wrong. You know the bar isn't paying you to be there right? You don't have to impress them. Oh THE GIRLS? That's why you're dressing up? To impress them? Of course! Because drunk girls have SUCH HIGH STANDARDS! You're a handsome fella. Just smile a lot and no one will notice that you're wearing a city league softball t-shirt.

Ignore Her: Going out *just* to pick up chicks is super creepy, but if you're gonna do it, at least be smooth about it: Ignore her. If you ignore that girl and just have a good time, it'll drive her crazy. While you're busy playing darts and laughing at your buddy's jokes, she's busy thinking *What must be wrong with me that's keeping him from creepily touching my arm every time he says how interesting my tanning salon job is??* If there's one thing a girl hates, its people having a good time that doesn't involve her gyrating hips or barely-covered breasts...and we all know there's a thin line between "hates" and "sleeps with out of confusion"

WHAT DID YOU SAY??? My friend Tim recently told me he knows he's getting old because "screaming over house music at a chick that has no clue who Marty McFly is no longer seems worth it." This is a good sign that you're a grown up. I don't *do* house music. I'm not cool enough to fist pump. Do you know why? BECAUSE NO ONE IS. It's not cool. It's not handsome. It's silly. And not a funny, ironic kind of silly either. It's silly like watching *The Notebook* with a girl: You're probably doing it to impress her, but it's painful to watch and she's not gonna want to sleep with you after seeing it.

Have a seat: Why are you still going to bars that don't have enough tables? My idea of a good Saturday night isn't standing around holding all of my stuff for a few hours. Give me a table. I don't want to worry about spilling my water because the guy in the pressed shirt had too many Jager bombs and can't stand up straight. I'm a grown-up. I don't like standing in groups of people unless we're huddling to chant the losing team's name after we destroy them in softball, or if I'm waiting in line for a super hero movie. Grown-up shit. This should also let you know the caliber of girls you have around: if you're in a bar where you have to stand all night, and she's wearing 4-inch heels that she keeps complaining about, she's probably not a Harvard grad. Which brings me to our next point:

Drunk girls: There comes a point in any man's life when drunk girls stop being attractive...wait scratch that, drunk girls were never attractive. There comes a point in a man's life when he's not willing to get drunk enough to *tolerate* drunk girls. And yes, I understand that we've all been the annoying drunk a time or two...but it's time to grow up. You're a handsome fella and vomit is a bad color on you. This mindset is easy to achieve; just adjust your timeline a little bit. Go out at 6pm after work. Happy hour prices are better, the girls aren't shouting "wooooo!" or trying to stick a cigarette-scented tongue in your mouth, and you'll be awake in time to enjoy Saturday morning cartoons. And who knows? If you're lucky, you'll have met a nice, normal, non-glitter-stained girl to watch cartoons with you.

Last Call: This seems to be the toughest concept for guys to do away with. You don't HAVE to shut the place down every night. Go home. Have you ever been outside a crowded club SOBER at closing time? It's the most depressing thing ever. It's like speed dating...well...it's like speed dating *without* the nametags...and the only question is "can I touch your vagina?" What, you're hoping to find a winner in the patrols of skanks that are still there at 2:20 AM? All you're going to find is the self-respect that they dropped on the sidewalk...right next to yours.

But hey, if you're the 30-year-old dude who's still hitting the clubs every night, I won't judge you...but mostly because I'm going to be in bed by then.

- *Chapter Ten* -

Sitting at the Kid's Table: The Handsome Man's Guide to Weddings

It's no secret that I'm oozing with childlike wonder. If you don't believe me, ask my Lego collection. If it doesn't answer, that's because you *don't* share my childlike wonder and lack the imagination to make Legos talk...I feel sorry for you.

But sometimes even I have to put aside childish things. This is America. We have to grow up, get jobs, pay bills, etc. It's a cruel world out there and you gotta get yours.

I think Winston Churchill summed it up best when he said "Cash rules everything around me. C.R.E.A.M. Get the money. Dollar, dollar bill y'all".

And I realize that much of this book is dedicated to helping handsome men act like a grownup, but sometimes, you need a refresher course to acting like a child. There's nothing wrong with it. In fact, it's part of this balanced breakfast like a Poptart or maybe Coco Crispies...or Fruity Pebbles...Are you sufficiently lost now? Great, time to move on.

The Point:

I'm about to go to a wedding. They're a great couple and I couldn't be happier for them. But also, I'm happy because weddings are a time when you can put aside your adult impulses, and just enjoy life for a moment. Here are the top ten ways to pull that corporate-issued stick out of your ass and enjoy a wedding for what it is: a party.

1. **The Kids Table:** If you have the chance, sit at the kids table...even for just a second while you're holding your girlfriend's purse as she powders her nose *again*. Kids are cool. They won't judge you, they'll ask you easy questions that you know the answers to, and they know the tricks to take over the stage in the Zombie level of COD. Sitting at the kids table is the best reminder of what's important in life...namely: magic. If you can pull a quarter out of someone's ear: you're a hero. And also you're like ten times bigger than them so you can feel hella superior. Oh, and use big words, they hate that...wait I'm getting off track: Sorry, I was bullied a lot when I was little. Don't be mean to the kids. Just enjoy their company and their sweet sweet X-Box knowledge.
2. **The Electric Slide:** A few years ago, I was DJing my friend Megan's wedding and *NO ONE* knew the Electric Slide. Did this stop me? Not at all. I left the iTunes playlist I'd set up weeks before and twisted a couple dials on my pre-amp so it looked like I was actually doing something...and then I hit the dance floor. I grabbed

Megan's grandma by the hand (honestly this probably isn't true...it was just a random old lady that I assumed was her grandma but she could have been a caterer for all I know) and pulled her out on the dance floor. We started boogieing. If you've never boogied, than you're not even allowed at my wedding (Sorry ladies, this premise is doubtful: I'm like Jason Bourne or Jack Bauer: I work alone...and I kill terrorists...okay no I don't but the "alone" thing? Totally me). Soon, everyone joined in. That's the power of the Electric Slide my friends. It's magical.

3. **Tie-loosening:** This is a concept that may be foreign to you. Do you wear a suit and tie to work every day? Possibly. Do you roll your sleeves up on a daily basis? Maybe...but do you ever loosen your tie to a ridiculous extent? Doubtful. At a wedding this is encouraged. As the night races on, loosening your tie is the physical equivalent of telling the party "things are about to get sooooooo awesome in here!" Nothing screams *party* like a loose tie...except maybe the drunk uncle who will inevitably wind up sitting in the middle of the dance floor actually screaming "party!" while grabbing at Brides Maid's dresses. Which leads me to point No. 4:

4. **Bridesmaids:** I know, I know...*Wedding Crashers* made this a cliché point, but I'd be remiss if I didn't mention them. My theory around bridesmaids differs from that movie though: I don't see them as easy targets that are vulnerable because they're not the ones getting married. I just think girls have more fun when they get dressed up in a pretty outfit. This makes em way more prone to electric sliding with you, and isn't that why we're all here anyway?

5. **Drunk Best-Man Speeches:** Have you ever seen one of these go wrong? It's great. What a Best Man's Speech *should* look like is this: "<*insert a short heartfelt toast to the bride and groom and how great they are*

together>" but here's what they *usually* look like: "*<insert a long, awkward, drunken rant about the crazy times they had back at the frat house that he laughs at throughout because he thinks he's a comedian>*". IT'S GREAT! Nothing is more entertaining than a person who doesn't understand the importance of contextual protocol. Also, if this happens: watch the change on the faces of the bridesmaids that may have planned on taking him back to their hotel jacuzzi tub before he opened his mouth.

6. **Recent Divorcees:** These women are always on their Cindi Lauper. They're at the wedding but want to forget *all* about marriage or anything related, so if you're a single guy, they'll be happy to Electric Slide with you and buy you drinks while you tell jokes that make them feel 21 again. And it's all harmless fun because she's not gonna get all clingy like human girls do.

7. **The eventual moment where the DJ plays something wildly inappropriate and your parents are flying too high to even notice that they're dancing to "The Thong Song":** Yeah I don't even know how to elaborate more on this. But it's awesome. Something about a dance floor at a wedding makes old people forget that other people can see them, and they don't understand this new music anyway so they stopped trying to listen to the words years ago.

8. **The drunk members of the wedding party who sneak off to bust slobs in a bathroom stall because they don't think their father noticed but he did...he did:** Nothing's better than watching someone get caught in the act by their whole family. It gives you a sense of joy you didn't know possible. TRUST ME. You'll feel like you're 12 again.

9. **The Buffet:** Have you ever seen a kid at a buffet line? He doesn't know what to do with himself. It's the Disneyland of eating. That's because he's not on Atkins, he's not

watching his figure and he's not even "trying to save room for cake"...he's just doing what feels good. We could all use a little more of that right ladies? (I don't know what I threw in the "ladies" part at the end there...I think its fun to be creepy sometimes).
10. **The ring-bearer inevitably break-dancing:** This kid is awesome. Get out there and pop-and-lock with him. He's going to *destroy* you in a battle, but that's just because he's got the "cute" factor. Don't be offended when we all clap for him instead.

I hope this gives you some helpful tips to regain your child-like wonder. That's an important part of being a handsome man. If not, let me know and you can come over and play Lego's with me. That always works.

- *Chapter Eleven* -

A Handsome Man's Guide to Staying Diverse by Finding a Black Friend

That title was a bit misleading, and I apologize for any racial unrest it may have caused. This post isn't about race, it's about *fashion*...because black guys are the MUST HAVE accessory for spring.

Black is the new black. If you didn't know that, you'd better ask a white girl.

In 2010, the hot item was the gay best friend, but with the end of "Don't Ask, Don't Tell", the edgy vibe that came from the gays is gone (you can tell because I didn't get all awkward when I said "the gays"). The new hotness is like a retro-throwback to 90s music: all about black dudes.

Now, having a black friend is exciting. *"Finally!"* you think to yourself. *"I'm gonna take him everywhere!"* But not so fast buddy. Like any accessory, you have to know the appropriate time to rock your new black friend. Not every black guy goes with every occasion, and you don't want to wind up at a dinner party in the Hamptons sportin' business casual when it's a formal occasion. There are several types of black guy, and I'll help you decide which one is right for you:

The Formal Black Guy: This is your best bet for company parties, weddings or any other formal event. The formal black guy goes best with events that involve impressing your girlfriend's father or to show those jerks who made fun of you in high school how cool you are now...

"Even white dads love me," says Tim Bowman, my resident black guy expert. "They always say 'I'm one of the good ones' which is racist but who cares I'm sleeping with what he created."

Now, once you get a few drinks? Ties get loose and things get awesome. Sometimes the Kid 'N Play Dance gets broken out. This is your best bet for a wingman because chicks dig black guys and...well...chicks dig a suit.

Pair with: Your own suit, but not a black suit because that's probably what he's wearing. If he's wearing a colorful suit, you need a new formal black guy because you accidentally got yourself a pimp.

The Trendy Night Club Black Guy: Trying to impress a girl? The Trendy Night Club Black Guy is the one for you.

He gives you that "I'm cool enough to hang out with black people, but not the scary ones so you're safe. Plus, I must be really super awesome to know him right? Look how trendy he is! He's wearing a vest and tie *with blue jeans!*" vibe.

"Everyone loves trendy black guy!" says Tim. "Because I'm black, but minus the rage. The tie makes me approachable like a butler or a valet or someone else who works for your racist grandpa."

Girls will see that and think "man, this white guy's *soo* urban! I should sex him up a little bit."

Pair with: A two-day scruff and a shirt with dragons on it.

The hipster black guy: This is good if you don't want to scare your white friends. It says "yeah I'm accepting, but I really don't *get* their culture." With the hipster black guy, *you don't have to!*

He's in a rock band and played intramural lacrosse in college. He's basically you with a tan!

"If you can tolerate the fact that I like everything you do but in an ironic way, I'm cool to hang out with," says Tim. "And *Kanye says so...THAT'S* why I wear scarves dude!"

He's good at dive bars with college chicks because they're stupid enough to think he's hood, and he's smart enough to let them think that.

Pair with: a T-Shirt and jeans...Just not ones with holes in them...that's his look!

The scary black guy: This is only good in very specific circumstances.

If you decide to pick up this model, keep in mind that your other accessories may not go with it. House parties in the suburbs, college bars, places where white people feel safe. He'll make them uncomfortable, but then you can swoop in and seem "dangerous but sweet" for hanging with this scary guy and then defusing the situation.

"Give me your goddamn wallet before I do whatever it is you're afraid I'll do to your wife and daughter, white boy!" says Tim. "I MISS the days of NWA. You guys are getting too comfortable."

Pair with: a cocky attitude and a smile…also, good shoes and a clean right hook because for some reason, white guys always want to fight him.

- Chapter Twelve -

Maxed Out: The Handsome Man's Gym Warning

Remember when men were men? They were strong from building things and fighting wars and eating giant legs of mutton off the bone?

What happened to all the MEN? Am I right ladies? It must be *so hard* to find a good one.

Okay enough of this touchy feely crap. In fact, THAT'S the problem these days. Guys are too in touch with their sensitive side...They're *SO* in touch with their sensitive side that they don't even know what to do with *your* sensitive side.

Fellas: The correct way to handle her sensitive side is a 3-part process as follows:

1. Put on The Delfonics "Didn't I Blow Your Mind This Time"

2. Blow her mind...

3. Remind her that you just blew her mind.

*if you don't recognize that song, ask your dad to bring out the LP...because you were most likely conceived to it...Then ask him to explain to you what an "LP" is.

The *incorrect* way to handle it would be...oh I don't know...to hear the words "sensitive side" and think "damn I'd better get to LA Fitness and work the shit outta my sensitive side!"

That's the root of today's problem. Guys are posting more Facebook profile pictures from their bathroom mirror than girls are.

A HANDSOME MAN DOESN'T NEED THE WORLD TO KNOW HE HAS ABS! His washboard stomach with that little ridge thing like D'Angelo had in the *How Does it Feel* video should be a surprise.

You know what? It should be like in *Super Mario Brothers* when you get the invisible "?" with a hidden life in it: The lady should be excited when she stumbles upon it.

So I enlisted the help of two outspoken friends. Kelsi and Taylor, both attractive, athletic young phillies who no doubt have gym memberships, but liberally use the word "douche" for guys who have gym memberships. Together we've put together a list of things you should stop doing to live up to your responsibility as a handsome man. Why? Because it's fun to make fun of you.

YOUR HARDCORE WORKOUT HABITS ARE MAKING YOU SOFT

1. Check-ins from the gym: A Foursquare check-in is like saying "I want to remind you all that I need attention, but I have nothing interesting to say"...yes I've used it before, shut up this isn't about me. But at cool places like when I checked in from the top of Mt. Everest or Kelly Kapowski's bedroom. If you're checking in, wouldn't you only do it because you want people to be jealous of where you are? I'm never jealous of LA Fitness or Gold's Gym. I hate both. There are too many people like you getting in the way of weight racks because they're busy checking themselves in on Foursquare....This is not man stuff.

2. Status Updates from the gym: The status update from the gym is the check-in's retarded cousin from Alabama. Why? Because we have to hear you *talk* about your workout. I'll leave the rest to Taylor:

Taylor's Take: *They act like they are changing their iPod, but are actually writing "get it right, get it tight", "getting my mind off things", or "tworking out" on a Facebook wall. This is the same douche who posts pictures of his grilled chicken breast when he gets home from spotting the douche in the affliction shirt.*

3. Michelob Ultra and a grilled chicken breast: We get it...a real beer will make you balloon up like Val Kilmer, but having 13 of those when you don't have a single carb in your system to soak it up is going to make you more of a drunken douchebag than your sweet, sweet pecks will make up for.

4. Self-Love: Ahhh the male version of the duck face (we'll get to this later...stay tuned). Guys have been posting shirtless bathroom mirror pictures since the days of Myspace. You know, in ancient times, seeing someone's abs meant they were poor.

Think about it. "Look at how good my body looks" is the least manly thing ever implied by a photograph...so congrats fellas, you've outdone the duck-face chicks.

Kelsi Says Stop: *These guys are trying to get noticed as super "sexy/hot" and that they are "manly and buff" when in reality girls look at those pics and think the guys are way too in love with themselves to possibly love any other person...But other GUYS look at it and think "I can bench more/my arms look bigger/better."*

So unless that's your target audience, might be time to take it easy.

5. Talking...just stop talking: I could sit here and tell you about how annoying it is to have a dude come up in the middle of your set and tell you what he's working today and how much he repped out, but I'M WEARING HEADPHONES SO YOU SHOULD KNOW THAT MEANS I DON'T WANT TO TALK TO YOU.

6. Recognition is overrated: I automatically assume the worst in someone who posts their gym routine on Facebook...Even other douchebags can't *possibly* take the time to read through that can they? What's the point? Here's a hint fellas: girls aren't impressed by this...Don't believe me? Take it from the girls (they're girls):

Kelsi Says Stop: *These guys need to be recognized for anything positive they are doing with their lives....which sadly is limited to the gym. Like "Oh I went for a run today and benched 300lbs 5 times." which says "I am so awesome, I deserve a huge pat on the back". I mean, if you are battling ninjas it's one thing...then you do deserve a pat on the back, and probably an ass-squeeze too.*

Taylor's Take: *Ahh the "I work out harder than you" guy who always tells you how to do it "properly" even though one bicep is larger than the other from jerkin it because no one wants to sleep with a know-it-all.*

Take this knowledge and channel it into fitting your 3-hour work out into 45-minutes like an adult so you have time to go eat a cheeseburger and enjoy a second or two of life.

- Chapter Thirteen -

Recession-Proof Elitism: A Handsome Man's Guide to a Down Economy

Look guys, I don't pretend to have all the answers...I don't have to, because I *DO* have all the answers.

Let's all be honest here...you're not reading this because I *don't* know what I'm talking about. I'm better than you are. You can tell from the way I dress (Docker's flat-front wrinkle-free khakis, all day every day) to the way I live (in a fashion you could call "trendy", "urban" or "ballin-outta-control"), and even the company I keep (my friends are probably way cooler than yours and the girls we hang out with are like 10x prettier).

Okay, now that I've officially insulted you, do you see what I did there? I made sure you knew I was better than you. You know how much it cost me? Not a cent. It's a recession folks: Frugality is crucial, but so is appearance. In these trying times, it's important to be vigilant of this, and constantly search our souls for new ways to show people that we're better than they are. Are you up to the challenge? Then come along like a newborn lion cub in a Disney movie while I take you around this great big African prairie we call "life".

How to Keep Your Swagger in a Down-Economy

Okay, for those of you over 35: "swagger" is a combination of a person's *style* and *confident attitude*. Also, why the hell are you reading this? You should be working. I'm still in my 20's, it's okay for me to slack off but you're a grown up and should start acting like one.

...Did you buy any of that? Because you shouldn't. You're probably going to get laid off soon anyway. You're old, so I imagine you work for a non-tech-related company that will probably go bankrupt soon. You don't even know what cloud-based computing is. What good are you in this modern world of ours? Unless you're cool. Then you can stay.

The point I'm trying to make is this: Recession-Proof Elitism is a lesson for EVERYONE, not just the handsome man. We all need to learn to be awesome despite an empty wallet. Here's how you do it:

1. Give up dreams of a nice condo in new skyscraper downtown: Sure those are nice, but you're not going for nice: you're going for cool. When was the last time recessed lighting got you laid huh? Never. What you need to do is find yourself a shitty flat in an old brick building in an old part of town (for Seattleites, these can be found in the Pioneer Square or SODO neighborhoods...also, how lame is the name "Seattleites" huh? I vote we change that). You can rent a shitty brick place with gates on all the windows to keep your crack head neighbors out for less than HALF the rent of your nice skyscraper in a secure building with "working plumbing". Now, the most important features you're gonna want to look for are these:

- Exposed brick walls: These are key. They seem really trendy, but old shitholes have them too. You can hang awful paintings on them and point a track light from ikea at the painting. You'll act like you *know* art and give people smug looks like they have no clue. Let me know if you need any shitty paintings: I specialize in them.
- A bedframe that sits low to the ground: They make these at ikea also. It looks SUPER trendy and it's basically just a sheet of plywood on a box that you throw your mattress on top of. Chicks love these. Also, when you have an exposed brick "loft", you don't have to have a bedroom, so when you invite a girl over, she's already next to your bed. At that point you're on your own but it should be an easy transition if you have the next important piece:
- An ipod player with some Smokey Robinson queued up. You turn that on, and suddenly your dark, cold apartment seems like you have it that way on purpose.
- Any of the following things are extra credit points: overflowing bookshelves (half-priced books sells old legal books "by the yard" so you can stock it with important looking shit you'll never read), an easel (this way you can say YOU painted the shitty paintings on your wall), an old camera (it doesn't have to work, it's just so it looks like you have a deep sensitive and artistic side), and of course, a stocked wine rack with dusty bottles so it looks like you're "saving" them for special occasions (just keep a box of Franzia in your fridge and you'll be good).

2. Hang out in a trendy coffee shop: NOT STARBUCKS. I can't stress this enough.

A.) Because I miss the Sonics.

B.) Because you can't be better than everyone if you're drinking the same coffee they are.

What you need to do is find some little corner coffee shop that has a super hipster vibe to it. Someplace that snacks of communism like is the best. Spend as much time there on your laptop as possible. Pretend you're a writer. The best way to pretend you're a writer is to start a humor blog. It gives you a reason to slack off, and it also gives you a feeling of self-importance, and that's what we're trying to accomplish here. The coolest part about these trendy coffee shops is that you can buy an 89-cent cup of joe and then drink their trendy water from the spouted glass cooler thing that has cucumbers and limes and junk in it.

3. Trade in the SUV for a bus pass and a bicycle: Sure, the *real* reason you're broke is because you got your second DUI and aren't allowed to drive for two years anyway, but that doesn't matter. You live downtown and you're *way* greener than everyone you work with. You're committed to the cause man. Good for you!

4. Develop an affinity for a very specific dive bar: This is key. If you have a favorite bar, you're not expected to go anywhere else. People will come there to see you, which automatically puts you in an elitist position of control. And if you have your own *dive bar*, you can just chill there and drink dollar Rainiers until you know the bartender well enough to get them for free (I miss you Bill).

5. Go to art gallery openings: These are the best. They're free, they happen all the time and you get wine and cheese. You should always pretend like you know the artist. He'll be too smug and drugged up to say that he *doesn't* know you anyway. Don't bring a date. Bringing a date makes it seem like the *only* reason you did it was to save some cash. If you go alone, you can hit on the other artsy chicks there and seem like you're the cool James Dean loner type.

6. Buy a Kindle: Sure, spending money like this seems counter-intuitive, but you have to look at this like an investment: If you have a kindle, you're clearly smart and up on the current trends. Plus, since you'll be riding the bus a lot, you need something to separate yourself from the homeless people who have also read this book and will be looking trendier by the day.

7. Date a grad student: This works for both men and women. When you're dating someone in grad school, no one expects either of you to have money, because you're working toward something greater. Even if you have no plans of doing anything greater. It's that association that matters. That being said, as soon as they're done with school, they'll be in more debt than several small countries, so you need to cut bait and run.

8. Find some kind of cause: Finding your own cause to champion can be tough. What do you pick? A woman's right to choose? AIDS? Hunger in Africa? Getting the show "Firefly" back on the air? It's up to you. But you have to stand by your cause like its Robin Williams in Dead Poets Society. This is your new identity. Every conversation, passing comment or joke is a person's unspoken way of asking you to tell them why they're a bad person for not caring as much as you do.

9. Renounce your religion: This seems to be the new trend. Not believing in anything means you're smarter than the rest of us. If you don't believe in God, it's because your brain operates at a higher function than mine because you saw through that whole "Virgin Mary" conspiracy that I clearly couldn't. But you can't just choose not to believe in stuff, you have to tell the rest of us why we're wrong, and do it in as condescending of a way possible. After all: you saw the *DaVinci Code*.

10. Borrow a friend's dog and sit around reading in the park: It's free, so you've got that going for you. Also, chicks go to parks bro. If they see you sitting there reading your kindle with a yellow lab resting on your lap, they'll stop their jog and come over to pet it. Then you can point out that you're re-reading Voltaire (I always assume someone's smart when they're reading a book for the second time. Because it means they *really want it to sink in this time* or some other logic that's *way* beyond my comprehension).

11. THIS IS THE MOST IMPORTANT STEP: Buy yourself some Dockers flat-front khakis: This is an investment I support. Trust me, anytime I see someone in these pants I think "that dude's got it figured out. He knows how to live" and I try to be friends with him. Usually he won't, and he thinks it's weird that I asked, but that's just because he's so much better than me. And better than you. Unless you have some Dockers flat-front khakis. Then you're on his level too.

You've got a full life ahead of you, don't waste it on mediocrity.

- Chapter Fourteen -

Have You Thanked a Gay Guy Today?

It's time for us to say "thank you" to the community that helped us become the handsome men we are:

It's time for us to thank the gays. I'm serious. All of us. Even you. Find one in your office and say "Hey gay guy, thanks bro"...he'll be the trendy one in Italian loafers and French cuffs (this is a very narrow stereotype and I apologize...there are SOOO many more stereotypes I don't have time to mention).

Thank him for that chick you hooked up with last night. Thank him for your wife. Thank him for helping you find that inner strength to be the real you (the entire state of Alabama just told me to fuck off).

No, I'm not just saying that because there are more women to pick from when the rest of the dudes are pairing off...although that's awesome too.

And no, I'm not just saying that because it's nice when the guy who can sing, dance, cook, decorate, knows all the best floral arrangements AND is sitting in the corner chattin' up your girl turns out to be gay.

You should thank them because the gays have made floral arrangements a tool for straight guys (I can say that, right? "The gays"? Is that allowed? It feels dirty like saying "the blacks").

I was having a conversation with a girl about this last night (not a real conversation with a real face-to-face person, mind you. What am I...eighty? This was on Twitter). She informed me that "things that aren't considered manly by societal standards earn you triple bonus points with the ladies."

So thank you gays. The road you paved must have scuffed your Italian loafers...but thank you. Thank you for making all the things I enjoy "cool" now.

Super-Hetero Disclaimer: I also like welding bridges out of steel and shooting bandits in the old west. These are just some of the many way-straight things I do on a daily basis.

In the 80s, there were three things that were cool: Money, sports, and cocaine (and the piano key neck tie, but I associate that with cocaine anyway). Now there's a new cool. And chicks finally dig it. I don't mean "oh that one chick who goes against the grain and won't join the cheerleading squad because of ideological differences" either. I mean the majority. They all seem to want a guy who's totally, 100% *a guy* but also likes a lot of the stuff that your divorced alcoholic uncle would call *gay*.

If You're A Handsome Man in the Modern World: Thank The Gays

- In this new era, it's okay that a guy like me can play football all day, and then come home to paint, write or cook a nice grilled tilapia with mango cilantro salsa and a jalapeno aioli...in fact, he'll probably get lucky (from a *chick! SCORE!*). And for that we thank you gays.

- In this brave new world, it's FINE that a man wears jeans that fit AND listens to rap music. In fact, girls now dig pants that fit. They're 56% more likely to try to get you out of pants that fit than ones already hanging off your ass. Thank you gays.

- In this post-homophopocalyptic age (which is a word I just invented that combines homophobic and post-apocalyptic...you're welcome world), it's FINE for a fella to sip a nice Bordeaux while he pisses off his balcony because he's drunk from the previous 12 Bordeaux's. Thanks gays.

- In this modern metropolis, there's nothing wrong with a guy hanging an artistic photograph of an abandoned country farm house under his newly-installed recessed lighting while he watches the HBO Saturday Night Fights. Chicks dig a versatile man and its okay to have a little class. Thank you for pounding this lesson home gays...you know...figuratively.

- In any major city, thank you for previously dilapidated neighborhoods becoming "arts centers" where cute hipster chicks in black framed glasses are usually single because they've been hanging out with...well...you guys. Thanks gays, and keep bringing those girls around.

- And finally, in this world filled with all sorts of madness and hypocrisy, thank you for convincing liberal chicks everywhere that traditional marriages haven't been held to the sanctimonious standards they were spoon-fed as children so they'll leave me alone about "commitment" for a few minutes at a time because you gently pointed out that shows like "The Bachelorette" exist. Thank you gays…from the bottom of my heart.

Just know that handsome straight guys out here are pulling for you handsome gay guys and your BASIC CIVIL RIGHT to develop shitty VH1 shows about gay celebrities who sleep with a bunch of contestants and then eventually settle down with one of them for a week or two…because it's not Adam and Steve: It's Ray J and LaQuanda, Stephanie, Rachelle, Tiffany, Amber, Jolene and Amy. *Remember that.*

Part II

Pretending You Care

- *Chapter Fifteen* -

Pretending You Care: A Handsome Man's Guide to Corporate Life

I don't know if you know this about me, but I'm SUPER talented. It's true. I'm pretty much awesome at everything. I dance like a combination of Fred Astaire and Channing Tatum, sing like Katy Perry's breasts, I always get the girl (she was probably yours…sorry about that), and I recite French poetry with President Obama during halftime of our basketball games at Rucker Park. I'm even better at dreaming than you (last night, I was Batman at a party with my friends in the Florida Keys and we stopped a drug-smuggling ring…your children can thank me later).

But the most impressive thing about me? Well…aside from my sweet calf muscles, I'd have to say my childlike wonder. If you don't have childlike wonder, you're really missing out, because it's *delightful*. I don't think it's a secret that I'm "a child". My friend Tim and I once took girls on a double date to the movie *Sky High*...which we'd already seen...twice (needless to say, those relationships were short-lived).

First of all, Sky High was awesome so check your tone at the door. Second of all, I realize that I'm what some people would call "an adult" now and I should probably "grow up" or at least "pretend to" and maybe "learn when a sentence is over and it's time to move onto the next thing".

Even with my childlike wonder, I've become super-good at pretending to be an adult. I have to. I work in an adult office with other adults...well, and that one guy in tech support with the four-foot-tall Star Wars Imperial Walker, but he won't let me play with it so he doesn't count.

I know there are probably others out there who pretend to be an adult, and since I'm the best at it, I figured I'd give you some of my tricks. This list is highly sensitive and classified and you should keep it a secret (that's why I put it in a book).

How a handsome man pretends he's an adult at work:

- Wear a collared shirt and roll the sleeves up: Rolling the sleeve up is a time-honored symbol that says "Dang y'all, I'm workin' *way* too hard for sleeves today!"
- Carry folders and stacks of paper around. It doesn't really matter what's in it. If you carry a folder with this week's "Spiderman" in it, people will assume it's a folder full of spreadsheets. To this day I don't know how to read a spreadsheet, nor do I know what one actually is, but I carry a stack with me wherever I go.
- Walk fast when you're on your way back from a three-hour lunch. When you look like you're going somewhere, no one questions where you've been (also, eat food while

you're walking around. It looks like you were too busy working hard and being a grownup to take a lunch).
- Get a two-monitor system. If you have two monitors, you can have 82 things open at once. This allows you to pretend like you're looking at pie charts and bar graphs while you email your friends Youtube links.
- Furrow your brow. I can't stress this one enough. Nothing says "I'm not working" like a giggle. If you're reading a funny Facebook status, look at it like it's a math problem. This way people will think you're doing market research on social networking practices.
- Also: use words like "market research" and "social networking practices"
- Sleep with a co-worker. This one seems counter-productive, but it gives you a counterpart that you can trust. You can schedule meetings with this person so it looks like you're doing stuff (make sure you book a conference room in outlook for these "meetings"). Also, when the inevitable break-up and workplace drama happens, you have an excuse to say "It was all those late nights at the office"...and that's pretty cool.
- This one is a little embarrassing, but poop a lot: This gives you an excuse to get away from your desk and play a couple levels of "Angry Birds" a few times a day.
- Drink a lot of coffee. It makes you jittery. People assume when you're jittery that you're just stressed...you know...from all the working. Plus, it gives you an excuse to stand up a lot.
- Under-promise and over-deliver. You've heard your bosses say this before, so use it. When you're about to do a project that takes 15-minutes, say it will take an hour and a half. This will give you a lot of time to play Angry Birds on the toilet.
- If there's one piece of advice that I want you to take away from this, it's to write a book. I'm serious. You can do it at work. Right now, my brow is furrowed like crazy, my

sleeves are rolled up and my desk is a mess. I'm typing like mad. Salesforce.com is opened on my second screen and there are three excel spreadsheets about things that my company apparently does strewn about my desk. If you're always typing, you're too busy to talk, which is good because once you open your mouth, they're going to realize that you don't have any idea what it is that you "do" for a living.

I hope this list helps you as much as it helps me. If you'd like, put it into an excel spreadsheet and tack it to your cubicle wall. It'll look official and let's be honest; no one really knows how to read those things anyway.

- Chapter Sixteen -

Seven Habits of Highly Effective Handsome Men

I often get asked the question, "Hey Kevin, how do you find time to be so awesome? You give us hilariously insightful blogs, podcasts and books, are a super awesome friend to everyone you know, a pillar of your local community, a *Godsend* to all women AND you somehow have time for a day job!"

The secret is easy: I set *super* low expectations at work.

It makes it pretty easy to slack off when the standard for your quality of work only takes 15-minutes a day to maintain (HR Department: I'm kidding of course, I work hella hard on…you know…websites or whatever it is we do around here…I'm totally not writing this while I'm at work either you guys, despite my use of the word "here" that implied I'm at the office now…I'm not).

There is something important that you should have picked up on in that last paragraph: I said *hard on*. But also, I've learned how important it is to be *effective*. It's the key to everything in business, from being a strong and successful part of the American workforce, to being an unnoticed and lazy part of the American workforce.

More important than effectiveness in work is effectiveness in *life*...And I do that too.

How do I do it? Well my friends, I've outlined that in this highly effective chapter (*way* more highlier effective than that stupid book), and I won't waste any more of your time, because that would be ineffective...much like Luke and Han Solo in *Return of the Jedi* when they let some little teddy bears capture them with sticks even though they had blasters, a light saber, an R2 Unit, modern technology and THE GODDAMN FORCE! What a waste of time! They had a galaxy to save! Did they really have that half-a-day to spare? No!

Do you see what I mean??? Han and Luke just wasted *another* 15-seconds of your time by making me point out how ridiculous that whole scenario was. They clearly didn't read this post.

THE SEVEN HABITS OF WAY HIGHLIER EFFECTIVE HANDSOME MEN

1. **Don't Read Full Books About Being Effective:** How long does it take to read a book about being effective? If you did it in one sitting, I'd estimate 147 hours (he uses a lot of big words). How did he even fill that many pages with seven steps??? Those steps are way too long! **Better option:** Just read this chapter. It's great. You're done in ten minutes...then you can play Mario Cart or something. Remember that this is the age of Twitter: 140 characters

is all you remember anyway, so reading that whole book is a terrible life decision...WAY worse than that time you hooked up with a homeless hippie at Burning Man. Reading *this* entire book? Way better of a decision, but if you already paid for it, I don't really give a shit what you do with it.

2. **Play video games:** Do you play video games? No? Well maybe you should. What did you do today? Talk to a couple clients and write a company-wide memo? That's cute. I used the genetically engineered powers that The Umbrella Corporation gave me to thwart their evil plans and save a bus-load of people from zombies! Video games give you goals and aspirations. Nothing is more productive than a mission. Your boss can yell at you about documenting your last voicemail in salesforce.com, but he can't take away the victory you just had over the Nazi Zombies.

3. **Baseball Caps and Flip Flops:** Welcome to the West Coast. You may think we're just "lazy" or "carefree" but in actuality we're just way more efficient than you. I'm wearing a baseball cap and flip flops today and I just got out of a meeting with a guy from Detroit who's with the advertising agency for Cadillac. Sure, he's more "successful" than me and maybe he's "smarter" but let me ask you this, how long did it take him to gel up his hair and put socks on this morning? Probably longer than it took for me to throw on a Detroit Tigers cap and flip flops. PS: I didn't wear the Detroit hat to suck up or anything; I'm just a huge Magnum P.I. fan.

4. **Get Married:** This is awesome advice for men AND women. You're welcome. Marriage saves SOO much time! You don't have to go out to bars anymore (I'm told this is why most of you go to bars), you won't have to keep a drawer full of clothes over at your girlfriends house (having things in two places is highly ineffective), and you can have kids so you get to have an excuse to keep toys

around (you won't have to explain your Lego collection to girls anymore. That takes up WAY too much time that could be spent watching *Game of Thrones*).

Guys: Date and marry women with daddy issues. She won't expect much and will want to keep you happy so you won't waste any unnecessary time on "foreplay" or "cooking your own meals."

Girls: Just find yourself a rich 89-year-old dude. He'll die soon and then you can be happy and rich, which is *super* effective

5. **Get a pair of Dockers Flat-Front "No Iron" Khakis:** Imagine how much time you'll save once you don't have to iron pants! There was a study last week that said 100% of people who wear Dockers Flat Front "No Iron" Khakis are 75% MORE effective than guys with pleats. That's just good sense.
6. **Screw the sixth habit:** It was a waste of your time and that's hella ineffective so I deleted it.
7. **Delegate:** This is important. No one ever argues with delegation if it's phrased right. Don't *ask* your coworker if they "would mind taking over the Powerpoint for tomorrow's meeting." That's stupid and ineffective. Instead, just walk quickly by their desk and say "Yo you need to do the powerpoint for that meeting tomorrow. I emailed you the outline. Thanks." This accomplishes many things:

A. You're walking fast, which is super effective.

B. You don't have to do that stuff anymore. This gives you more time to be effective on www.ESPN.com or even better, www.kevinsaysthings.com.

C. You just established yourself as the Alpha Male. What's more effective than being a badass? If you didn't answer "nothing" than you need to read this one outloud in the mirror every morning. Don't worry though; you're weak and because of that are probably alone...so it won't embarrass you in front of a girl/boy who spent the night.

8. **Since you skipped the sixth habit, develop an eighth:** Eight habits are more effective than 7. Suck it DOCTOR.

- Chapter Seventeen -

A Handsome Man is Never THAT Coworker

It was like love at first sight...but only if "love" means "a strong desire to avoid that person on a daily basis because their presence offends all eight of my senses. Yes, I said I have eight of them...step your game up Bruce Willis."

If that's somehow *not* the definition of love (hard to believe), then I guess what I'm trying to say is this:

Sometimes, co-workers are really thoughtful and make it immediately and blatantly obvious that you should never be friends with them.

You know the ones I'm talking about. When you pass them in the lobby, you duck out the smoker's door to avoid the off-chance that they'll try to tag along for lunch. When they open their mouth in meetings, you automatically roll your eyes and stop paying attention. When you see them out in public you give a disclaimer to your friends between gritted teeth:

Oh shit, okay guys this is that annoying chick from work I was telling you about. Be cool and maybe she'll go away.

But then again, maybe you don't have that co-worker...Maybe *YOU ARE* that co-worker. So, at the risk of sounding like a bad Jeff Foxworthy bit that he became a multi-millionaire off of (actually I'm okay with that risk), here's a list of things I've always wanted to say to *THAT* coworker. Hopefully these will help you not be that coworker...because a handsome man is better than that.

Are You THAT Co-Worker?

- **Dear overly enthusiastic coworker:** saying "you know what's crazy?" before everything you say *doesn't make it crazy*. "You know what's crazy? My West Virginia dealer got 250 visits to his mobile site last month" doesn't make sense because it's not crazy. Next time you preface a statement with "You know what's crazy?" you'd better follow it with something like "My dragon ate my hamster's sword and then puked all over my collection of robot dwarves"
- **Dear cubicle decorating coworker:** sometimes actions speak louder than words. Like the pictures of your cats in your cubicle that say "lets never be friends" WAY louder than saying "lets never be friends" ever could.
- **Dear loud talking girl who keeps getting dumped:** You should stop complaining that the guy you're dating is only with you for sex...you probably have a shitty personality; otherwise he wouldn't mind talking to you with clothes on. Fix yourself.

- **Dear Girl In The Breakroom Talking Too Loud For Me To Enjoy My Cinnamon Apple Oatmeal:** Justifying the d-bag you're dating by saying he's nice when "it's just the two of you" is like sharing a needle with another junkie because YOU don't have AIDS: It's only a matter of time.
- **Dear Coworkers with Kids:** No, I don't want to buy wrapping paper to support your daughter's school. And not just because I don't know her: I won't buy anything because you bogarted the coffee machine while you wasted my time. Some courtesy would have skyrocketed Lil Suzie to the next prize level which is probably an awesome razor scooter. Maybe you teach her some work ethic and have her go door-to-door like the Good Lord intended
- **Dear Dog-owning coworkers:** Why do you decide that we all have to sit around petting it for an hour? Strippers don't even get this kind of attention.
- **Dear "I make you feel awkward about my weight" coworker:** Coming to work with a giant Latte and Danish every morning and then spending the day complaining about how you can't lose weight is like meeting a guy at a dirty bar and complaining about the STD he gives you: You set yourself up for failure. Either be fat or be skinny. No one cares.
- **Dear bad-email-etiquette coworker:** Emoticons in work emails are not okay. Can we all just agree that the winking face emoticon ;) means "I'm not confident that you picked up on my sarcasm because I'm stupid. I don't understand how to use words and/or punctuation, and even though I would never wink at you in person, this seems acceptable"? Also can we agree "LOL" after your own comment means "What I just said was stupid but I figure if I digitally laugh, you might join in and not notice I'm retarded"?

- **Dear "Guy running the meeting I'm ignoring":** NO guy-running-this-boring-ass-meeting, I DON'T know the best way to optimize a contact page to demonstrate security. You can CLEARLY see that I'm over here writing a chapter about annoying coworkers and haven't been paying attention. I have no clue what you've been talking about. Watch your mouth and don't be so smug.
- **Dear Account Executives:** Telling me about how big your commission check was last month is like a girl saying "I don't normally do this" when she goes home with a random sleezy dude. A.) He knows you're lying. B.) He doesn't care.
- **Dear Girl Who Likes to Hear Herself Talk:** First of all...do girls only compliment the way each other look so they can swing the conversation back to themselves? "You look soooo good today. I wish I looked like you. Ugh! I look all blotchy because my cover-up wasn't working right this morning". Second of all: blaming the way you look on makeup is like me saying "My cynical attitude is only an issue because my coffee hasn't kicked in yet". Own up to it. I'm an asshole. You're ugly.
- **Dear "Bring my club clothes to work" coworker:** Remember the other day? You had your hair and makeup all did and a little black dress. I saw you in the hall and said "Aw you look cute"...You got mad that I said "cute" instead of "hot"...This frustrated me because A. we're at work and B. I thought it was a stretch when I called you "cute".
- **Dear bitching and moaning coworker:** A fair warning...Whenever someone starts complaining about "workload" in a meeting, I want to hit them in the face with a Bible. Not because I have a strong sense of irony and believe that God or Lil Baby Jesus wouldn't approve of their attitude or anything; just because the Bible is a huge book and it would get them to stop talking so we can move on with the meeting better than a paperback copy

of Grisham's "The Client" would. Oh you have a lot of work to do at work, do you? That must be why they give you a paycheck.

- **Dear Nerd:** I just made the mistake of playing with the AT-AT (the robot camel things from Star Wars for you non-Star Wars fans) model that you have next to your desk. New rule: Don't bring toys into the office if I can't play with them. That's like a girl inviting you up after a date and saying "let's just talk"...don't invite me up then. I was cool at the door...I was gonna go home and watch Mad Men.
- **Dear used-to-be-pretty girl I sometimes ride the elevator with at work:** your smoker's cough I never noticed, gum-smacking habit that was cute til today and newly acquired fake orange tan just totally killed my good mood...Sigh...that was like going home to eat your leftovers from an awesome meal and finding our your roommate took 'em. Thanks for eating my leftovers. Love, Kevin.
- **Dear coworker who should be buying me a cookie right now:** If I have headphones in, and you start talking to me and I don't take them off, you should definitely be offended. It's kind of a dick move. But you should also stop and think "Oh hey, he's probably listening to Sam Cooke and that's a really sexy thing to do, I should leave him alone to be awesome" and then you should feel so bad that you buy me a cookie...chocolate chip.

Dear handsome friends: I can only hope that my cynicism can help you avoid further embarrassment from being *that* coworker. Love, Kevin.

- *Chapter Eighteen* -

A Handsome Man's Guide to the Apocalypse

-or-

Throwing your office safety coordinator to the zombies

Sometimes, it's important for a Handsome Man to have a game plan. Sometimes he's gotta be prepared...and sometimes it's important for him to take a break from reality and write a chapter about zombies.

With all the talk about the "End of Days" that's supposed to happen in 2012 (according to a race of people that is so smart they don't even exist anymore), I've spent a lot of time looking around my office and thinking about what any good Catholic is thinking about: Zombies.

Are you ready for the zombie apocalypse? The rapture is boring. Angels are just coming down and taking the good and holy people up to Heaven. The rest of us get to stay here and party for another 1,000 years. The zombies however...they'll take

EVERYONE. Are you ready for that? More importantly...ARE YOUR CO-WORKERS?

There was a report released recently about a fungus that's getting into the brains of ants and controlling their thought patterns. It makes them hungry for a specific type of leaf, and it makes them violent and agro. That shit is terrifying. If you're not terrified, it's because you're not smart enough to understand what this means. Tell me, how long before the fungus gets into *human* brains and changes it's hunger from "leafy greens" to "human flesh"?

The answer you're looking for is "not long".

And tell me, where do you spend most of your time? In your office. Sitting in a cubicle. Staring at a computer screen.

That's what I'm doing right now! There could be a zombie apocalypse going on in the streets 10 floors below, and if I didn't stay on top of the zombie blog pulse (which I do) I'd have no clue! Neither would my coworkers who I'm looking around at...and I've gotta tell you: I'm not sure they're gonna make it.

OFFICE POLITICS IN A POST-POLITICAL WORLD (AKA: WHEN ZOMBIES ATTACK)

- **Rule No. 1:** When zombies attack, there are no rules. Your boss isn't your boss anymore. Remember, in this anarchy he is no longer calling the shots. In fact he's old, slow and doesn't know he's one life-or-death decision away from being used for bait in your Zombie-killing trap. He's just a guy with a laser pointer now (also, steal his laser pointer...those things are sweet) This is awesome to think about unless you're the boss. Personally, I'm stronger and smarter than most of my bosses, so I'll naturally assume a leadership role when this happens...plus I keep a samurai sword under my desk (HR: No I don't)(Everyone Else: shhhhhhh). Your boss will fight you on this because they're used to leading the pack, but their experience lies in compiling website metrics and analyzing spreadsheets. If yours lies in being super badass and not being a nerd, it's time to take over.

- **Rule No. 2:** During the apocalypse, past entanglements will be your natural basis for emotional allegiance. Fight this thought process at all cost. Just because you slept with Gina, your VP's assistant, at the Christmas party last year, it doesn't mean you have to protect her. She's weak, whiny and will probably continue to ask where this relationship is going while we fight back a flesh-eating zombie horde made up of ex-mailroom clerks. Use her assumption against her in a pinch. Hit her with a stapler and throw her to the zombies. I know she's obnoxiously skinny, but her gamey frame should buy you enough time to shoot the fire extinguisher you put in her purse while she wasn't looking (also, who carries a purse during a zombie attack? She deserved to die). Thank you Gina: My future family will light a candle for you for saving the life of their patriarch...although I'll change the story to make me seem heroic.

- **Rule No. 3**: Fear does strange things to people. You'll be tempted to create an alliance with the people you used to work closely with. **Don't do this!** These people aren't equipped to handle this crisis. You really think the guy who listens to ABBA on his headphones all day is ready to fight zombies? How about the girl who plasters her cube wall with pictures of cats? She can't pull the trigger in a pinch! What you need to do is go to IT, snatch their best guy, and make him your right hand man. He knows about your building, knows how to fix things, and probably has a key to the roof. Plus, in the case that this all blows over, you have a friend who can hook you up with a 36-inch monitor. Next, go down and grab the security guard from the front desk. He's not supposed to carry a gun, but if every movie I've ever seen is correct, he carries one anyway because he's got his fifth attempt at the police academy entrance exam on Sunday (where do you think I got the gun to shoot the fire extinguisher in Gina's purse? This isn't a half-assed guide! Take it seriously!). Then grab the janitor. He's got a third set of keys and access to cleaning agents and astringents and other chemicals that you can make fire bombs and Molotov cocktails out of. Plus, turn a mop into a spear. It's a primitive weapon, but it's also going to be badass when you get to use it.

- **Rule No. 4:** This isn't a movie! If someone gets bitten, kill them immediately! These are *work friends*. Is there anybody there that you would really have a moral dilemma about shooting an arrow through their head? And look...I don't know how you got a bow and arrows at work but somehow in a zombie infestation situation one guy always has one (*disclaimer to my coworkers in the case of a lawsuit and/or zombie apocalypse where I need your allegiance until I can use you as bait: I'm just kidding. You guys are the shit and I would DIE for all of you!*).
- **Rule No. 5:** Attack or Fortify? This seems like a tough decision, and it really can depend on your office. If you work downtown: Fortify. Chances are you have a Starbucks in the lobby anyway, and I bet there are enough calories in one of their "cake pops" to feed the building for a week. You have dozens of floors to work with. Also, you have air ducts and might get to hide out in one with a lighter wearing a wife beater like Bruce Willis and say "Let's get together, have a few laughs" which is the most badass thing you can do in any situation, let alone a zombie apocalypse.
- **Rule No. 6:** Avoid Conference Rooms. Conference rooms are a corporate "dead end"...But you should steal the video projectors to use as diversions. Zombies are

attracted to movement...its science. Cubicles are safer bets: Use the cubicle rows to create intricate loops. You get to use them as cover while you hide and shoot zombies, plus you can outrun and outmaneuver them. This is good if you're trying to lose a couple of slower teammates: The loops will tire them out. You can also funnel the zombies into a trap using the cubicles (and using the slow co-workers...they're like cheese...annoying cheese that doesn't understand why no one wants to hear them complain about how "it's Monday" every Monday. Get over it. AND STOP EATING FISH AT YOUR DESK! If it smells, you have a responsibility to take it to the cafeteria).
- **Rule No. 7:** Call of Duty Players: DO NOT GO BACK TO REVIVE BITTEN TEAMMATES! They're out til the next round.

Look, I'm not saying these tips will save your life: That's up to YOU. But if you can use this to mentally prepare, you're chance of living just went up a million percent, and in the new world, my kingdom will need good looking people like yourselves. You're welcome friends. Now, back to reality.

- Chapter Nineteen -

Just Quit: The Key to Finding a Badass Job That Chicks Dig

I'd imagine you're sitting in an oversized arm chair next to a giant fireplace with a snifter of brandy and reading this chapter on the Kindle app of your iPad 2 while your wife and butler check to make sure the maid didn't steal any of her diamonds during her rounds.

No? You're not doing *any* of those things? Sigh...me neither. I'm sitting in a cubicle with a spread sheet on my second screen in case my boss walks by.

The dark side of being poor...okay pretty much all of it.

Weren't we supposed to be ROLLIN in cash by now? That's why I went to college! So I could get the Dockers Flat Front Khakis, get a sweet job, find a trophy wife and roll around in a Bentley on 24s! Do you mean to tell me I'm spending half my paycheck on college loans for *nothing?*

The not quite as dark side, but still pretty dark, just because "dark" is badass:

Now before you fall into a depression so deep that you can't dig yourself out with a shovel made of Zolof, you should know something: It could get *so* much worse...you could be alone in this world without your helpful guide Kevin to say things that inspire you to be better than you are.

That's right; you have me. And even though you're stuck in a dead-end job sitting in a cubicle collating numbers all day (I don't even know what that means), you have options. I'm going to help you get out of there and find your dream job. Let me be your guidance councilor.

- Will this dream job make you rich beyond your wildest dreams? Not at all.
- Will it set you up for a nice comfy retirement? Negative ghostrider.
- Will it help you pull chicks? I'm not gonna lie to you...absolutely. TIME TO FACE FACTS MY FRIEND: Your plan failed. Let's try ol' uncle Kevin's path.

How to Quit Your Job and Find a New One That Chicks Can Dig

Step 1: Quit your job. I'll wait....did you do it yet? Good. See how easy that was?

Step 2: Freak out for a second because you didn't line up anything new ahead of time. What were you thinking? That was irresponsible!

Step 3: Accept the fact that your new lifestyle will include a lot of activity that can be described as "irresponsible"...then embrace it. It's dirty and sexy...and chewy. You're gonna love it.

Step 4: Take a job doing something dirty, irresponsible and sexy.

And now you're set. Chicks are gonna be all over you bro.

But Kevin, I don't know where to look for one of these jobs! What do they look like? Where do I find one? ARE THERE EVEN JOBS IN THIS ECONOMY???

You sound like a chick. Calm down. It's not like anyone *told* you to quit your job. I mean, other than me.

Yes. There are jobs you can find out there. In fact, most of the jobs I'm talking about, you don't even have to apply for, you just start doing them.

"Cool" Jobs That Chicks Dig

Drummer for a Band: It doesn't matter if you're in a Cat Stevens cover band...chicks love drummers. Sure, you'll only work shitty bar mitzvahs and hippie weddings and stuff, but when babes ask what you do, you can say "I'm in a band." Plus you can wear leather vests with no shirt on...no one else in America is allowed to wear leather vests!

Artist: Let me tell you, I've been pretending to be an artist for *years*. I splash some paint on a canvas every now and then, sell it to some schmuck (unless you've bought one of them...that was my best one ever), and call it a day. Chicks dig artists for their sensitivity, but you can't say *why* you're sensitive. Let her know there's pain in your life, but don't let her know that it's just a sliver in your thumb from climbing trees last weekend.

Bartender: This one's pretty simple. Do you know what the best pick up line *ever* is? "What can I getcha?" When you're the one pouring Mango-tinis down her throat all night, she's bound to fall in love. You've listened to all her problems, smiled really big at everything she said... She'll want to marry you...or just get drunk off Mango-tinis and take you to pound town.

Dog Walker: If there's one thing we know, it's that bitches love dog walkers. So do the ladies. Say you've got a couple little pooches in the park...Maybe a cute little breezy is out for a nice jog...maybe Buster "accidentally" gets off his leash and runs up to her. Maybe it's adorable. Maybe she winds up putting her tongue in your mouth by the fountain.

Peace Corps: You care so much about helping people that you quit your job to volunteer full time? Were her clothes still on after you finished telling her that? Didn't think so...And another upside: oh weird, this last week of freaky-deaky fun has been great, but I'm getting deployed to Nicaragua to feed starving children. No cell service. I'll *totally* call you when I get back.

Door Man at a Trendy Night Club: Lets be honest, this dude is always kind of a douche, but he's GOD to skanky club rats. Girls will sleep with a VIP host just to *get* to the door man so they can sleep with him to get into a club that's usually free. This guy's favorite line: "Sorry we're at capacity."

I'd help you apply for one of these gigs, but I've got a gallery opening for my new show "smiley faces with crayons"...It's ironic because I'm coloring sad faces. Chicks dig irony they don't understand.

- *Chapter Twenty* -

10 Things a Handsome Man Should Do Before Quitting His Job

You guys, I have a story to tell you:

I was feeling awesome this morning. I got out of bed, and while I was singing my morning "the sun is coming up" song like I do every morning while I dance around my bedroom, some freakin bluebirds and a deer fixed my bed for me and made me delicious pulp-free Florida orange juice. Then I took a shower (even though I magically smell like roses and a meadow after a spring rain anyway), brushed my teeth, left my hair how it was because it just looks sexy naturally, threw on some jeans and tennis shoes and headed out the door.

On the bus, like 37 girls were fighting over who got to sit next to me, and I can't really blame them, I didn't shave this morning so I looked like I belong on the cover of GQ instead of the #3 Metro. The girl who won the fight, sat down, and I pulled a fake Lee Press-on nail out of her skull for her, said "what's up sweet thang?" and she fainted...I was okay with it because I was listening to John Legend's "Slow Dance" which is too sexy to be interrupted by a chick who's out of breath from fighting.

Then I got to work...and I sat down feeling good. I got my cup of Gloria's coffee that has a hint of chocolate in it, and sat down at my desk...looked around my cubicle with a smile on my face...and realized I want to quit my job.

Don't be all that surprised, A. I just wrote a chapter about the jobs that are way cooler than this one, and B. does anyone *really* enjoy their job? If you do, you probably don't work in a cubicle, and if you work in a cubicle and *still* like your job? You're the lady with pictures of cats hanging from branches plastered on her wall.

And so I sat around thinking about quitting my job, but then I realized there was so much more I want to accomplish here...and no, I don't mean "close the Anderson deal" or "create a company-wide policy that fosters growth and innovation"...my goals and dreams are *way* bigger and more important than that. So I give you this list:

THE TEN THINGS EVERY HANDSOME MAN SHOULD DO BEFORE THEY QUIT THEIR JOB

1. **Set Up Your Office Enemy:** Everyone has a nemesis...someone whom you deeply despise. They hate you too don't they? I mean, if Cheryl didn't hate you, why would she have snitched about your two-hour lunches and leaving early every day? Cheryl needs to pay. If you're quitting and have turned in your two-week notice, this is the time to do just that...Here's my advice: After Cheryl

goes home tonight; use her computer to steal hundreds of thousands of dollars from your company. I don't know exactly how to do this, so you're gonna need to enlist the help of an Asian or Indian guy (they'll have the software you need). Then use the money to buy a bunch 60-inch TVs and Bose stereo equipment and have it delivered to Cheryl's house. The company will find out, she'll get fired AND be humiliated AND have to sell the TVs and stereo at a discounted price on craigslist so you can get a really good deal.

2. **Get Fired:** This is the best way to quit. Usually it's because you did something you weren't supposed to. Like write a book while you're at work and on your company computer with a chapter about how much you want to quit your job. Then hope that someone in HR reads it and causes a big hullaballoo (PS: I spelled that right on the first try). Why do you want to get fired? Because if you quit you can't collect unemployment and you have to turn in a two-week notice. If you get fired, you just stop going, collect your final check (with your vaca balance too) and start collecting that sweet, sweet government cash.

3. **Get Creepy With the Young, Tan, Blonde Receptionist:** I know you've been toying with the idea for months anyway...Don't even sweat it. Chances are she's Russian, listens to techno and likes super creepy guys anyway. She'll probably be flattered. **Or if you're a girl:** He's a guy and he's been imagining you naked anyway.

4. **Get even creepier with all the single, 30+ brunette professional attaché-carrying hotties:** They're just happy you're talking to them. These girls go out for happy hour every day because they're afraid of ending up alone and want to numb the pain, so just make sure you're there for the next one so she can play the "I want to invite you back to my place but I don't want you to think I'm that kind of girl" as she runs her

stiletto up your thigh under the table like this is *Gremlins 2*. **Or if you're a girl:** He's a guy and he's been imagining you naked anyway.

5. **Get the creepiest with your boss's hot teenage daughter that he stupidly brought into work:** (See #3). **Or if you're a girl:** He's a guy...no wait, actually you should see #3 too.

6. **Do parkour in all the places that you have dreamed of in the last year:** Do a sweet 360 off your bosses desk, a jump kick off the statue in the lobby and try to run across the water in the fountain out front...like Jesus (Most of his miracles were legit, but in this case, he was just super good at parkour...that was a type-o in the Bible).

7. **Steal Awards and Leave Ransom Notes:** Most companies have won awards from some organization that says they're "The best place to work in Seattle" or "America's Top 40 For Customer Service!" and if they've won these awards, they probably got trophies and plaques. Steal these and leave a ransom note demanding a piranha aquarium in the lobby and NWA's "Straight Outta Compton" to be played on repeat over the intercom for the next three days. It's probably their policy to not negotiate with terrorists...but just maybe you'll get lucky. Plus its fun cutting the ransom note letters out of magazines.

8. **Throw a Party on the Roof:** My office is in Downtown Seattle and has a 360 view of the City, the Sound, The Olympics, The Cascades, Mt. Rainier and both stadiums. When I quit, I'm throwing a kegger on the roof. Tiki torches and a roasting pig...and I'm hiring Keith Sweat to perform because he seems like he's probably out of money by now.

9. **Re-Arrange Everyone's Food in the Breakroom Fridge:** People take this fridge too seriously. Put Susan's left-over beef stroganoff in Steve's lunchbox and then

leave a note on his lunch box that says "Thanks STEVE! Real mature!" I mean, if you're leaving, you might as well watch some office drama unfold. Just sit back and get yourself some popcorn...I think Andrea has some in her lunch bag.

10. **Jerry Maguire Walk-Out Style:** On your last day, throw a huge fit. Take the pihrana that they put in the lobby when *someone* held their trophies ransom, make a big stink about how much you've given to the company and how excited you are to start your own firm or something...then see if you can convince anyone else to quit. It'll be awesome in the moment, and also, it'll be super funny when you later tell them that you already accepted a contract job at Google and you were just kidding. What an IDIOT!

Here's to quitting! I hope you have as much fun as I will!

- Chapter Twenty One -

Unemployment Means More Time to Be Handsome

I quit my job yesterday (how convenient for the progression of this book!).

I didn't quit because it was a bad job. It's actually a really good job...for someone else.

And not because I disliked my coworkers...Well, except you SHEILA.

I quit because working in a cubicle for a giant corporation was sucking my soul out through my headset and I was worried it would eventually manifest itself in my PC and start a digital dictatorship like TRON. Rumor is that's how Salesforce.com was started.

There comes a point in any man's life where he'd rather be poor and destitute than a sellout...Wait scratch that...that's silly. Being poor sucks. But selling out only makes sense past a certain tax bracket. I haven't reached that bracket yet and selling out for 50k a year is like punching puppies to support PETA....Both are awesome.

LOL I'm just kidding you guys. Both are awful. I just wanted you to make a disgusted face when I said I support puppy-punching. Also, I just said LOL. I'm sorry about that. No I'm not LOL.

Where was I? Oh yeah...So quitting might not have been the most "responsible" decision, but let's be honest; I'm too pretty to be stuck in a cubicle. And let's be honest a second time; I'm irresponsible.

Irresponsibility aside, I like to make a habit of doing everything in the sexiest way possible. Unemployment is no exception. All unemployment means is that I have 40 extra hours each week to be awesome.

And I know an extra eight hours of being awesome each day can seem like a daunting challenge, but I have faith in you. And also, I'm here to help.

SIX WAYS A HANDSOME MAN CAN STAY COOL WHEN UNEMPLOYED

1. Hang out in coffee shops. Coffee shops are cool and trendy. If you don't believe me, just ask the other unemployed hipsters there. You can sit there with your laptop and convince yourself that you should be a writer. Write a book. If you've never written anything, you'll feel like you have a future in it. If you used to be a legit journalist and are clinging to some sort of hope that you can make a career out of your ability to bullshit, it's a good way to feel like you're still relevant. You can write about stupid and inane topics like "what to do if you're unemployed" or "how to pick up cute hipster coffee shop girls" and if you frown at the screen every now and then, the girl working behind the counter who complimented your t-shirt will look over and assume you're working on something important. On a side note, does anyone have a good pick-up line to use on the cute chick behind this counter?

2. Own your unemployment. Don't lie about it. You don't need to pretend like you have a great job. No woman wants to date a successful guy anyway. They want to date potential. The only thing they like more than a doctor is a fixer-upper. That way they can claim you and tell all their friends that they are SOLELY responsible for your eventual success. That's what happened with my ex. She was constantly trying to "fix" me. She had me dressing better and made me get a better job and I could tell it worked when her sister (who had ALWAYS ignored me) made out with me in an Applebee's bathroom...So yeah, maybe Christmas at their house was awkward, but my ex's sister and I have been really happy together. Now that I'm unemployed, I'm hoping that their friend Amy is looking for a project. Amy has a boat.

3. Go to the park. Do you know who hangs out at the park? Chicks. They go there with little kids that they nanny for...or maybe they're not even nannies and just have their own kids...I never thought to ask. Either way, they're bored as sin and looking for some entertainment. You're entertaining, aren't you? Of course you are Tiger.

4. Start taking pictures. Do you know how easy it is to be a good photographer? It's not. But do you know how easy it is to be a *bad* photographer? It's the easiest thing ever. The best part is that girls are stupid. Take an out-of-focus snapshot of a plant with the sun behind it and tell everyone on Facebook that you're "pursuing a career as a photographer"...you'll be swimming in a sea of stupid women by dinner. Also, you just set yourself up to do a half-naked photo shoot with any girl you've ever met. For every guy pretending to be a photographer, there are 14 women who think they're models because some guy pretending to be a photographer convinced her she looked like a young Brooke Shields.

5. Volunteer. Sorry I don't have any cute sarcasm about this one. You've got a lot of free time now; don't be a dick.

Oh sorry, I forgot to add that this is a good way to feel like you're better than everyone else. It gives you a false sense of unmerited importance. That's why I do it. I just wish the rest of America was as unselfish as I am.

6. Write a book. That's what I did.

Even if you found this at your friend's house, you should also buy one. I'm unemployed.

Trust me fellas: you need this book. Ladies: you too. Why? Because it will give you something to do the next time you find yourself unemployed.

Part III

Part III

Loving Chicks Who Love Handsome Men

- *Chapter Twenty Two* -

How a Handsome Man Can Score Mad Chicks

You know what women like? A sense of humor. That's what Cosmo says. The No. 1 thing women want is a sense of humor.

Sure...if you're awesome at it like me. But some of you aren't as good at being funny; you need a back-up plan. So here's a helpful list of other things you can choose to be good at to get the ladies.

1. Be good looking. If you don't have a sense of humor, this is the No. 1 thing you're going to need to work on. "But Kevin, how do I get good looking?" you might ask. And that's a good question. Luckily for you, I've been good looking since birth and I have some good advice for you. You may start taking notes now:

- **Have good-looking parents.** This is a great way to get good-looking. If you can make sure you have good-looking parents, then your job is half done. Try to do this. That's what I did and it's turned out great for me.
- **Look at other good-looking people around you, and make sure you're better looking than they are.** I do this every day. I look around my office, see a few good-looking people, and then I just start being better-looking than they are. This works great if you're willing to commit.
- **Dress well and groom yourself daily**...did you write that down? Then you're an IDIOT. This was a trick answer to see if you were paying attention. Have you seen Brad Pitt or Tom Brady? Or me? Proper grooming and a filthy-awesome wardrobe aren't important if you're good looking. You look amazing no matter what filth you're covered in. You should have known that, and if you didn't, you need to work on my second point:

2. Be smart (or at least appear to be). Clearly I can help you with this one, because I'm smart. Girls like a guy to be smarter than her so he can open pickle jars and stuff. Unfortunately, there's no way to teach you to be smart. Brains aren't developed like a finely-tuned set of calf muscles. Brains are something you're either born with or not. It's luck of the draw. I'm just luckier than you, and we'll get to that later.

But if you're *not* smart, there's plenty you can do to fake it:

- Wear glasses. Chicks automatically assume you're smart if you wear glasses.
- Carry around books, but don't read them. You never see smart people actually reading. Why? Because we realized a long time ago that reading is for suckers. But women still think that's part of it, so we carry the books around to fool them. It always works because they're so stupid.

- If there's one piece of wisdom I can impart on you, it's this: STOP TALKING. Have you ever noticed that the smartest guy in the room is never the one spouting off at the mouth? It's the dude who lets you fools debate the possibilities of Time Travel according to the principles set forth in "Timecop" while he's in the corner stealing your girl. *Point of Clarification: I'm the exception to this rule, as I can argue the legitimacy of Timcop time travel while stealing your girl at the same time.*

3. Be Rich. I know right? Seems simple enough. Chicks dig checks. The problem with this is that in order to be rich, you have to already be No. 1 and/or No. 2. The easiest way to skirt this rule is to have rich parents…but let's be honest, if that's the case; you're probably No. 1 and/or No. 2 by default. But don't fret, there are a few things you can do to get rich if you're ugly, dumb and have poor parents:

- Rob people
- Ask people for money on Youtube. This seems to be working lately.
- Get injured in an industrial oil spill and sue for damages.
- Play the creepy neighbor/landlord/janitor in a big-time Hollywood movie. Then you'll be typecast as that ugly creepy guy and you'll be set for life. Which leads me to my final point:

4. Be famous. This is the Trump Card. If you're famous, you can be ugly, dumb and poor and chicks will still jump on your bandwagon. Chances are this will be a self-fulfilling prophecy and soon you'll be rich as well.

I hope this helps. I know it must be hard being as un-appealing as you are, but trust me when I tell you that it gets better. I mean for me and the other handsome men out there…it gets better for us; you're probably screwed.

- Chapter Twenty Three -

Picking the Right Pic: What a girl's Facebook Photo says about her

Since this book is bound to be a timeless classic, you will be reading it year-round, but I need to explain to you that summer just started. I can tell because people are starting to declare their free agency. And I don't mean NFL players; I mean freshly single people. Congratulations you guys.

Personally, I went in the first-round of this year's draft, and I got my single contract early.

But if you're a late-round pick, you're just getting into the game and you should say goodbye to the couples you used to play charades with…you won't see them until the off-season (Off-season starts in October when it's cold enough for a boyfriend/girlfriend again).

So you're single! YES! Okay...so...Now what?

When you're in a couple, you don't spend a lot of time on Facebook. You don't have to. You don't really care what other people are doing. But now you should probably get back into the internet...it's gonna be huge soon, you'll see.

Plus fellas: it's a great place for a handsome, single dude to get the scouting report...and ladies, now that you're single, it's time to refresh that profile pic.

Your profile picture says more about you than you think.

WARNING: DEMEANING & SEXIST RANT COMING UP

When a dude gets freshly single, he goes through facebook like a kid goes through baseball cards. First you open the pack of Upper Deck or Fleer and flip through them really quick checking the ones you need or already have in your collection: "Got it, got it, need it, got it, need it, married, crazy, got it, need it."

Then we'll take a look at the stats for the players we don't recognize: "Engaged; in a relationship but it's complicated; in a relationship...single...bingo!"

But as we're flipping through these, there are certain tell-tale signs. Certain queues in the pictures that you might not notice, but we do...we do. And that's what can separate the Ken Griffey Jr. Rookie cards from the Ruben Rivera .216 lifetime average cards (If you're not a sports fan, and that makes no sense to you, replace Griffey with the really hot chick from *Transformers 3* and Rivera with *Precious*).

So here's your guide to Facebook Profile Pictures. I hope I include yours in this summary because I'd hate for some of you to feel un-insulted. Why is this just focused around women's pictures? Because handsome men don't NEED validation from their pictures...we try to get it by writing books.

WHAT YOUR PROFILE PICTURE SAYS ABOUT YOU: A REFERENCE GUIDE

PICTURE OF HER PET: My cat is so adorable! Look guys! No seriously...look.

What it says about her: It doesn't really matter...you scrolled right past this one when you saw it. Who even *likes* cats? I could say anything I want right now and it doesn't matter because you're already down to the next example...syphilis.

BATHROOM MIRROR PIC: You know the one. She's holding her cell phone and standing sideways so you can see a little booty and/or side-boob sticking out from under her sequin dress. She's also *invariably* making that duck-face kissy-lips that girls decided is cute.

What it says about her: She's pretty good looking, but nowhere NEAR as good-looking as she thinks she is. *Hey guys! I just spent three hours posing so I can see what I'll look like when we take pictures later, but I look so good I'll just do it myself. And don't worry that the phone is covering my face. NONE of you are looking there anyway! Now* **LIKE** *this picture so I feel good about the side-boob decision!*

FAR AWAY PIC: Standing on a hill or beach or near a waterfall. You rarely see these pictures taken in front of a Walmart or the Free Clinic in Whitecenter. She's posing by herself, arms stretched wide as if to say "I'm SOOO happy, look at how much more awesome this place is than where you are!"

What it says about her: She's probably way too active for you. Where is she in that photo? Istanbul? Yeah, you're reading a humor book.

GIANT GROUP SHOT OF HOT GIRLS: Usually in a bar, usually hammered. ALWAYS doing that half-squat with my hands on my knees like it's a high school cheerleading team yearbook photo.

What it says about her: She's usually the least attractive one in the picture. It's like a "magic eye" poster, you're supposed to get so caught up staring at all the pretty colors that you start to see a sailboat…but she's not a sailboat…she's a dingy.

WEDDING PHOTO: Posing with her husband in a tux and white dress…so beautiful. So in love.

What it says about her: Who cares? She's married. Next.

BABY PICTURE: Awwwww. How adorable. She scanned in a picture that her mom had of her from when she was a baby. Or maybe it's her niece. She's got a milk moustache. That's so silly.

What it says about her: Her biological clock is ticking. RUN! She already has monogrammed towels with your initials next to hers.

TINY BIKINI ON THE BEACH WITH A DUDE: Awww it's Whats-Her-Name with This-Week's-Mistake! Don't they look cute? All tan and sexy on the beach? Clearly they're gonna be together forever!

What it says about her: She's considering breaking up with him. Go through your 800 facebook friends and find me ONE happily married chick whose profile picture is a skimpy bikini. Happily married chicks don't need you gawking at them. Their husbands are givin' it to them on the regs. Girls don't post skin so you WON'T flirt with her. They do it so their options are open.

TINY BIKINI ON A BOAT WITH A GROUP OF FRIENDS: Usually drunk. Usually with some random guys that they don't actually like but tolerate because they have a boat and pay for dinner. Always in a skimpy bikini. Sometimes she'll have those cut-off jean shorts unbuttoned, which is one of the only ways to put more clothes on and look even sluttier.

What it says about her: I'm only here because he has a boat and I get to take bikini pics here rather than on land - which instantly makes me better than 90% of the other bikini clad facebook skanks. But if you give me ANY reason to not have to hang out with this douchebag, I'll jump at the first opportunity you throw at me (i.e. a bigger boat).

THERE YOU GO! Hopefully this chapter will help scroll through your Facebook friends and pick your summer crush...but more likely it just helped you waste 15 minutes of your day.

- Chapter Twenty Four -

The Handsome Man's Little Black (face)Book

Do you remember the 80s? I realize some of you weren't born yet, but that's no excuse! Play like a champion.

I was already eight when the 80s ended so I had a *crapload* of real-world experience by then. I'd already started a break dancing crew that got into battles in the subway systems of New York City, I was dating all three of the Budweiser girls and I was partying with Spud McKenzie on the regs.

The 80s were a free-for-all (if you treat Hollywood movies as accurate historical accounts...which I do). The 80s were all about Sex, Drugs, and Krush Grooves. Everyone was happy and rich.

During the 80s, there was something called "the little black book" in which dudes kept numbers of girls they'd met and/or wanted to get all tender with.

"But Kevin, why didn't they just add each other on Facebook?"

Well, mostly because the little black book was a status symbol…It was a point of pride for sleazy douchebags and witty sidekicks in romantic comedies. Also, the technology for Facebook wouldn't be developed for another 10-15 years. You're kinda dumb.

But you do bring up a good point, fictional-person-who-asked-that-completely-illogical-question-that-conveniently-set-the-foundation-for-this-post:

With Facebook, the art of "mackin" on girls is gone. Did you read my last chapter? Facebook has taken over the game! It's so far gone that the term "mackin" might not even be acceptable anymore. I don't know. It's been so long since I've macked. That's just because I'm lazy, but there's another problem I've noticed:

In this modern Facebook world, you don't need to express your interest in a girl. You don't even need to get her number. You can just wait for her to leave the party/bar, ask her friend her name and then look her up on Facebook the next day. From here, you can research her likes and interests, stalk her photos and scout for mutual friends…then BAM! Slowly mold yourself into the character you think she'd want through passive-aggressive status updates and comments. It's great right???

NO, YOU IDIOT! You're an awesome guy (I'm guessing here because you have great taste in books). You need to own that awesomeness. What happened to your confidence? Just be you.

She'll like that. And if she doesn't it's probably because she's got syphilis or something (what, you don't tell yourself stuff like that when you get shot down? Does wonders for the ego).

So it's time for you to sack up. Put on your Dockers Flat Front Khakis because we're going out on the town. I'm gonna re-insert you into the wild (re-insert sounds dirty...basically, I'm gonna teach you how to hit on girls again).

THE RETURN OF THE MACK: How to Hit On Chicks Without Facebook

- **Assess The Situation:** I know fellas...it's so *hard* to read women when they don't have their "interests" and "favorite quotes" pasted to their tube top, isn't it? Even worse, the only "relationship status" option is a wedding ring. So how do you know if she's ripe for the plucking? You assess. Be like Mick in *Crocodile Dundee II*, reading the tracks and learning about your prey (FYI: calling women "prey" is almost as degrading as asking if they're "ripe for the plucking"...you should avoid that). **Examples:** If she's hanging all over a guy and laughing a lot, she's clearly single; people in relationships don't touch each other when they're out...or smile. If she's with a bunch of ugly friends, it's because she's on the prowl and doesn't want any competition messin' with her game. If she's playing Big Buck Hunter and singing along to Warren G's "This DJ" in an Iron Man t-shirt, then FOR THE LOVE OF GOD stay away from her...because she's mine.
- **First Impression:** Sorry bro, there's no shirtless bathroom mirror profile pic of your abs in real life. You gotta make your own first impression. And hey, if you think the best bet is to take your shirt off in the bar, by all means... go to a different bar. A woman decides within the first 60-seconds whether or not she's into you. For

some people it happens quicker than that. *True story: I was still taking my first breath when the nurse asked me if I wanted to come over and "watch a movie" but don't count on these results; you don't have my smile and charisma.*

- **Approach:** No Friend Request button here...This is real life. You always hear the stories about how people saw each other from across a crowded room and it was "love at first sight"...About 97% of the time, this is because the guy looked at her, bit his lower lip and did the stanky leg in the middle of a party and/or conference room. Try it. Chicks dig the stanky leg. It works *every* time...97% of the time. If you're wearing a pair of Dockers Flat-Front Khakis, this will be easy. Pretty girls are naturally attracted to the pants. I believe it's because of their patented cotton/poly/pheromone blend technology.

- **Pick Up Lines:** You can't just "like" her Foursquare check-in at Cheesecake Factory and hope she notices. You gotta actually talk to her. Don't walk up to her and say "yo girl lemme get dem digits" unless you're at a Vanilla Ice tribute concert (in which case I recommend you fight a giant mutated snapping turtle and a wolf in the middle of the dance floor...the true fans will get it) but pretty much anything else is fair game. My point is this: It doesn't matter what you do as long as you start a conversation. That's why pick up lines actually work. You could walk up and say "I'm a little concerned with the US response to the recent outbreak of zombies in rural Montana. What do you think?" Now you're in a conversation. Sure she'll be confused, but wouldn't you rather talk about zombies than her boring-ass barista job anyway?

- **The ABCs:** At some point, you have close the deal. This party/bar will only let you stay here talking about aspirations and favorite 80s movies for so long. Ask for her number or if you can get a drink sometime...or if you're really confident and/or sleazy, just say "do you

125

want to come over and watch a movie?" which is the international code for "let's get naked".

Alright dudes. I hope this helps. Unfortunately, you'll have to actually talk to people instead of just clicking a "Facebook Share" button, but if it works, you'll be clicking HER Facebook share button (ewww).

- *Chapter Twenty Five* -

The Handsome Man's Guide to the Girl at the Bar

One of my favorite things in the world is watching chicks at the bar.

Wait, that sounds creepy. I don't mean in a "Squintz is pervin on a chick" kind of way...I just mean in a scientific study kind of way.

You see, a big part of being a handsome, successful, charming man (read: me) is understanding the world around you. You can't conquer the jungle until you understand it.

Also, and more importantly, "Squintz is pervin on a chick" was a *Sandlot* reference, and if you didn't get that, you need to watch that movie before I can teach you anything else. Also watch *Sky High*...there's not a lesson there; it's just a great movie.

But I digress. Let me get back on topic.

If you're a young man – perhaps freshly out of college, perhaps a few years out of college but still out at the bars drinking an inappropriate amount for your age –then you may not pick up on the tell-tale signs that a girl at the bar is giving you.

I've got a few years under my belt, and I'm no longer too busy doing shots and fist pumping at the bar to notice these things. Here's what your sober friends noticed about those girls while you were too drunk to pay attention.

WHAT SHE'S DRINKING SAYS A LOT ABOUT HER IF YOU LISTEN

1. Cosmo: This girl owns the *Sex in the City* books. Yes I said *books*. They make books. Those are real things that exist in real life. This girl has one goal: to marry rich. Luckily for you, this goal has become so blinding that she'll believe anything you say, so you may still have a shot. Unfortunately for you, she's an awful human being and you'll have to listen to her talk about what the other girls in the bar are wearing and why it's terrible...you know...because her sequin halter top was a great idea.

2. Vodka with a pineapple back: She's Asian. For some reason Asian girls love this drink. They also travel in packs so bring a few friends and think of a good opener. My friend Mike's opening line to girls around here is "Let me guess what type of Asian you are"...but then again he's Asian. If you're not, you shouldn't do that. However, Seattle was recently voted the

"Capital of white guys married to Asian girls" according to a poll that I just made up, so you can probably figure it out.

3. Beer: This is a tricky one...this can go both ways. Either she's a casual drinker who likes a good microbrew every now and then and can hang out at a football game once in a while...or she's got a serious beer gut going on because she's constantly playing beer pong and flip cup. She thinks that because she hangs out with guys all the time and has gone home with half of the people in this bar that she's the hottest thing around. She'll probably burp in your face and yell at you a few times before she breaks down crying over a karaoke song. Why? Because she's dead inside.

4. AMF: If she's drinking something blue or green or glowing or in a test tube, you should probably stay away. This girl is big on sharing her STDs. How do I know this? She's drinking something that tastes terrible and sugary...even to the girl drinking a cosmo. Why is she doing it? Because she wants to black out. If you're unaware, AMF stands for "Adios Mother Fucker" and it's sole purpose in life is to help her black out so when she wakes up in a random frat house two states away, she doesn't remember how much of a skank she became last night.

5. Lemondrop: This girl hates alcohol but loves getting drunk. She's probably shy and awkward until she takes that first swig, then she gets loud and obnoxious because she a psychological drunk: she convinces herself that she's more interesting than she was sober, so she starts to adopt that persona after the first sip. Although let's be honest: she's probably right... she was SUPER uninteresting when she was sober, and now? Now she's dry-humping a guy in the hallway by the restrooms.

6. Wine: This girl wants you to think she's classy and sophisticated but she owns the entire *Twilight* series and her "classy, sophisticated" attitude disappears as soon as she's at the bottom of that second bottle. Luckily she's got a full wine rack that's perennially stocked, so she'll have a third open before you're done with your first glass.

7. Vokka Cran: No, that wasn't a type-o. Girls who drink vodka on the regs always pronounce it "vokka" and talk about it like it's a puppy. "I just love my vokka it's always there when I need it!" You could call this a problem, but it's okay because they can really only continue like this for another couple years before they wake up with an accidental case of pregnancy because they were too drunk the day before to remember their birth control.

8. Whiskey Anything: This girl thinks she can outdrink you. She'll be very vocal about the fact that she can outdrink you, but what she doesn't realize is that she makes stupid claims when she drinks whiskey. Don't take her up on this bet. First of all, she's gonna get hammered and no one likes that. Second of all, you're gonna get hammered and no one likes that. Keep it classy.

9. Tequila: This girl will be topless in about 20-minutes. Why? No one knows. It's just how it works. Unfortunately, unless you're in the 1-in-64 Americans who can drink tequila like a gentleman, you're going to be too busy picking a fight with the guy in the affliction shirt to take a look at her boobies.

10. Anything a guy buys for her: This girl is the most insecure one in the bar. Leave her alone. She needs to work out her daddy issues.

Next time you go out, keep this in mind. Watch the girls, stay coherent and enjoy your night of scientific discovery. Stay classy my friends.

- Chapter Twenty Six -

How to Tell She's Into You (Talk to her Dummy!)

It should come as no surprise to you that almost every woman I've ever met has been into me. I've got it all; I'm rich, good-looking, outdoorsy AND funny, athletic AND smart, manly as shit but also sensitive...and most importantly? I'm good at lying to myself about characteristics I don't actually possess.

It's because of this that women are constantly coming onto me. It's getting a little ridiculous. I can barely walk down the street anymore without some breezie going "Hey kid, do you know what time it is?" It's like "DAMN LADY! I'm just trying to get a cup of coffee! Not get molested in the street!"

But I understand that this doesn't happen to all of you. Some of you guys can walk clear across town without having to deal with this. Because of that, you miss the signs when a woman IS actually interested. And that's where I can help.

How many times have you been pervin on a chick when you stopped and asked yourself "wait...is she feelin me like I'm feelin her?"

You see, there are several things a woman will do when she wants you to know that she's diggin ya Big Dog! First of all, she won't call you Big Dog. Second of all, it may be so subtle you don't even notice it. Third of all, you're welcome.

FIVE WAYS TO TELL IF SHE'S DIGGIN' YOUR STEEZE

1. DIRECT APPROACH: Just walk up to her and ask her.

This one is tricky. Mostly because you have to actually TALK to a woman...but it can be worth it. It's the easiest way to cut to the chase and be a human being who knows how to interact with other human beings. Handsome men aren't afraid of women.

2. FEELING IT OUT: Just walk up to her and talk to her.

Engage in a conversation. This one is also tough because you have to learn to express yourself without a Facebook status, but I think you can handle it Big Dog (PS: You can tell that I'm NOT interested in you because I just called you Big Dog).

3. FIND A FRIEND: Not comfortable just walking up to her?

Walk up to one of her friends and talk to her instead. Will this get you closer to the girl you were interested in? Probably not, but let's be honest; if you're seriously considering this, you're not interesting enough for her anyway...so stick with her homely friend.

4. BODY LANGUAGE: Just walk up to her and talk to her.

Haha I totally tricked you by labeling this one "Body Language". Here's a solid piece of advice if you haven't picked up on this chapter's theme yet: if you talk to her, you'll have a much better chance at seeing her naked, which sets me up perfectly for some kind of "body language" play-on-words that I can't think of just yet...give me a minute and I'll get it...

5. THE WAITING GAME: Okay, okay...I get it. The previous points have all suggested that you just walk up to a woman and talk to her...and let's be honest, that's not going to happen. You're shy and uncomfortable initiating a conversation, so it's time to play the waiting game. And by "waiting game" I mean "never developing a tongue that's fluent in her body language" (told you I'd get it).

Do you *get* the lesson of this chapter? Quit telling yourself that she's too good for you. Talk to her. You're a handsome fella so she was probably just looking over at you thinking about how she wants to talk to you with her clothes off.

- *Chapter Twenty Seven* -

Is She Crazy? (Answer: Probably)

I'd like to switch things up a little and tell you a story.

This morning, while heading up to a meeting in a building downtown, two girls got on the elevator in the middle of their conversation. They were cute, so naturally my ears perked up, and the first thing I heard was "I'm just sick of his drama."

...That's it. That's the end of the story. I stopped paying attention after that because she was *clearly* crazy.

So I got back to work and I realized that although I'm constantly saying awesome things about how you can meet/pick up/date/break up with women, I've neglected to help you identify a key demographic of women out there:

Crazy Chicks.

Sure I talk about them all the time on my website, and have already made countless references to them in this book, but I just realized how irresponsible it was to leave out a chapter on how to avoid them.

I guess crazy chicks are so engrained in my life that I forget you may not know what the warning signs look like. There are very specific traits and characteristics that you'll be able to notice immediately. My goal is to help you realize these signs, because the paperwork required in filing restraining orders? Ridiculous. Let me hold your hand and walk you through it like a small child.

Also, ladies: If any of these characteristics apply to you, this is a good opportunity to fix yourself.

CRAZY CHICKS: 6 EARLY WARNING SIGNS

1. She "hates drama": No she doesn't. She loves drama. You know who hates drama? People who never have to say "I hate drama". This girl probably posts things on Facebook like "drastic times call for drastic measures" every time her boyfriend is out past the curfew she gave him. Drastic times ACTUALLY call for a collected, measured and rational response. Watch out for this girl, because if you ever smile at another woman around her, she'll hold a box cutter to your femoral artery and make you swear it won't happen again.

2. Mom will LOVE you: If you're on your first or second date with a girl you've never seen naked, and she says "my mom will love you" then it's time to go postal...No I don't mean kill her you idiot...Good God you *belong* with a psycho chick! What I mean is go down to the post office and fill out a change of address form, because this girl just planned your future in her eyes. It involves four kids named Dylan, Kaitlin, Bryson and Elliot....Kaitlin plays the flute and the boys are into lacrosse and soccer...oh, and you drive a mini-van. No one wants that. People who *own* mini-vans are sitting around in a support group somewhere *right now* trying to figure out how they got hooked.

3. All her friends are guys: When a girl says she "gets along better with guys than girls" I assume it's because girls can't deal with her crazy ass, and all of her guy friends slept with her at one point in college and didn't have the heart to make her leave the next day....so she just stayed and since she'd been with every dude in the house, no one really claimed her and everyone just kind of accepted that she was there....Basically what I'm saying is that if she ever brings you to a party, you should probably assume that 90% of the people there have been inside her.

4. She has an ex-boyfriend: Okay look...we've all got a few exes. But most of us don't talk about them non-stop (I mean, I guess I do but do public jokes on the internet really count? Doesn't that just make me an asshole instead? Also, I never claimed any semblance of sanity in the first place so get off my back and let me get back to my point). If every story I tell you invokes the response "ugh my ex used to say that *all the time*" I'm basically just counting down the minutes until you "accidentally" take me to a bar that his "band" is playing at so he can "accidentally" see how "happy" we are together and yeah I put band in parenthesis because they play shitty music and I hope you're happy living in his van STEPHANIE!!! Wait...am I missing my own point on this one? Yes? Okay moving on.

5. She's NOT crazy! This is the most basic litmus test. On your first date, wait til she makes a joke or tells a story, and as you're responding, casually joke "OMG you're so crazy!"...if she chuckles and says "I know" then you might be in the clear, but if she says "TAKE IT BACK, I AM NOT!" then you know she's got a thick file in a high school councilor's office somewhere. The caveat to this test is that "I know" can just mean she's a sleeper cell and you won't know she's crazy until you're tied to the kitchen table with hot wax being poured on you and a hazing paddle being covered in KY.

6. I'm a HUGE football fan: If she's trying to convince you that she's into your hobbies on the first date, or seem like the "too cool and awesome to be real" chick, then she's probably lying to you. Girls are generally good liars. I mean, they get up and spend an hour turning their face and hair into a lie (don't get me wrong, we're grateful; I *like* being lied to...although I also like crazy chicks), but when they try to pretend they're a HUGE sports fan? Their house of cards collapses. That's because usually they lie about feelings. There are no stats in feelings. You don't have to remember a 16 game schedule or understand how the BCS Bowl system works...NO ONE can remember that, so if she pretends to, she's lying....you know what? As a general rule, if she says she knows more about football than you and ISN'T Erin Andrews, just assume she's lying. If she IS Erin Andrews? Congrats sir. You are a God among men and I have nothing left to teach you.

- Chapter Twenty Eight -

Profile of a Stalker: How to Find Crazy in a Haystack

Shhhhhh! Be verrrry verrry quiet!

I'm trying to keep a low profile as I write this chapter because I have a friend at my house hiding from a stalker.

Also, I wanted to say "be verrrrry verrry quiet" because I've been watching Loony Tunes and Elmer Fudd's accent is super fun to do. Try it.

I SAID TRY IT.

Done? Okay good, now back to stalkers.

My buddy got himself a clinger. They were "dating" for a month or so, and I put the word "dating" in "quotations" because real dating involves more "Hey lets go get something to eat in sweatpants" and less "The safe word is *Forrest Whitaker*". What they were doing is called "sexing each other up" and I promise I'm done with the quotes now.

From what my friend tells me, he assumed she was cool with the arrangement...but turns out he was wrong...DEAD WRONG.

You see, the other night he was out on an actual date that didn't have quotations around it, and was bringing this date back to his house. When they got there, this friend found out that the stalker was in his room, uninvited, and his roommate had failed to tell him.

Side Note: Major party foul on his roommate's part for not firing off a warning text but I need a more creative way to say "bro code" before I write anything about that.

My friend's problem is that he didn't see the symptoms of a stalker, and you might not either. If you're a handsome man, you've probably got a few out there right now.

Hell, if you're a girl, you might even have your OWN stalker-like tendencies that you don't know about. And that's why I'm here.

IS SHE A BORDERLINE STALKER?

1. BUG EYES: So you hook up with a girl. You don't do this very often because if you're reading this book, you're classy as shit, but it happened. And that's okay because you're a grownup and you do what you want. You spend the night, and you cuddle and spoon and do all that stuff. In the morning you wake up and open your eyes to catch her staring at you. She quickly closes her eyes and pretends to be asleep. Why is this a bad sign? SHE WAS WATCHING YOU SLEEP! If this has never happened to you, I don't know how else to explain this because it's terrifying and is the first sign of mental instability. If it HAS happened to you, you don't need me to explain it because you're busy curled up in the fetal position just thinking about it.

2. FRIEND FINDER: So you've been out with a girl once. You had a great time at dinner and met up with a few friends at a concert. You and your date bailed early and went back to your place to "play scrabble" which I put in quotes because I meant you guys got naked and totally didn't play scrabble. The next day, you're sitting at work thinking about how good of a time you had last night. You hate your job so you check your Facebook. She's already Facebook friends with EVERYONE from last night. It could be easy to assume "oh it's cool, she just really clicked with my friends because we have so much in common!" but we all know that's not true. She's anchoring herself. She figures that if she gets your friends on her side, you won't ever leave her. Little does she know that your friends didn't even remember who she is, they just saw a girl who's profile picture was a duck-faced cleavage shot in the bathroom mirror and thought "next time I'm bored I'm gonna try to sleep with that."

3. BAR HOPPER: This girl sees your Foursquare check-in on your Twitter account that you never even told her about. Magically she's at the same bar where you checked in. She'll pretend not to notice you at first, but if you look like you're having fun and she gets more than two drinks in her, you're about to experience 2-hours of angry staring from across the bar. I've seen this happen. The upside is that you know where she is so she's not back at your place rifling through your shit. Which brings us to:

4. COVERT OPS: She shows up unannounced at your house...even if you're not there. She says she was just waiting, but don't be fooled...That's when she goes through your stuff. Women have this crazy idea in their heads that a date or two entitles them to a piece of our privacy. It doesn't. I get it, you think we have something to hide. That's because we do! You're not my wife; I'm allowed to hide anything I want from you. It's the same reason you wear make-up and a push-up bra: We don't want you to see the real us just yet.

5. TAKE A HINT: If you've broken up and stopped calling, texting, responding to calls, commenting on Facebook posts and haven't even acknowledged her existence in the last few months but she still shows up unannounced, you're beyond help. You're a couple weeks from getting a gun-rack as a birthday present...and yes...that was a Wayne's World reference fo yo ass.

6. THE CALL/TEXT: Finally, and most importantly, if she reads this chapter and calls and/or texts you to ask if she's a stalker, then yes...she's a stalker. But she realizes it. And acceptance is the first step. The second step is for you to move and change you cell number because she'll never stop until she has your house surrounded like Mark Wahlberg in *Fear* yelling about how much she loves you as she tries to kill your family. ***Good luck!***

Enough about crazy chicks, I'm developing hives. Let's move on and talk about some of the women a handsome man DOES want in his life.

- Chapter Twenty Nine -

Pulling Hipster Chicks: Acting like You Care Even Less Than Her

Okay look, there's a really easy way to snag yourself a hipster chick, but it's a *super* underground method so you've probably never heard of it. I heard about it from this dude I know that runs a basement herb shop in Chinatown. His name is Chesterfield Nguyen, but it's not a big deal or anything man.

Before I can tell you how to snag hipster girls, you should probably get caught up on what a hipster girl is, because I *doubt* you have any clue whatsoever. It's a hard concept to pin down and only the really trendy people know about it. She's an elusive creature. Half-rocker, half-nerd, half-preppy...I know...that's three halves, which is something you can't possibly understand, but hey...it's whatever man.

Here are some easy ways to identify a hipster girl in the wild:

- She knows all the coolest concert venues that you've never heard of, and as soon as it gets popular, she calls it "so dead" and goes somewhere even dirtier.
- She wears black-framed glasses…even when she's asleep…She doesn't need them, and they're messing up her vision, but she got them at this *awesome* vintage shop on Broadway.
- She *hates* being called a "hipster girl".
- She *loves* cigarettes and gay guys. And it's not just her glasses; *all* her shit can be described as "vintage"
- She knows everyone and is way cooler than you…trust me, Chesterfield Nguyen told me.
- She knits her own scarves and hat, but wears them with skinny jeans and $400 boots.
- Her musical taste could be described as "shitty" but you're still convinced your lame for not *getting it*.
- She has those bangs that run straight across her forehead…but she had them *way* before everyone else, and now she says it's about time for a change…bangs are so dead.

Once you've identified your hipster girl…it's time to do your research. But don't bother trying to learn all the latest fashions and the coolest bars and clubs: she knows them. You know that place that just opened on The Ave? Of course you don't. She's friends with the owner and she already hates that place because it "lost its underground vibe".

The research you need to do is going to make you more hipster than her; but be careful, don't buy into the hype. It's really easy to fall into the hipster mind state. I did that once, but being a hipster is *soo* over…Okay now it's cool again.

What you need to do is make her think you're "up" on some stuff that she's not...luckily, this is easy because the more obscure your knowledge, the more legit it is.

Here are some examples of things you can look up on www.AskJeeves.com (www.AskJeeves.com is *soo* retro...Google is for squares).

- Learn the name of the band that played on the soundtrack of a cult classic foreign film and find out when and where they also opened up for Arcade Fire (every obscure band has opened for Arcade Fire at some point...not that you would know that).
- Get a pair of limited edition shoes from a shoe company no one's ever heard of that went out of business in the 70s. They're probably ugly as hell and will be expensive to find and buy, but hey...now you have a story about how "misunderstood" the owner of the company was. *WARNING: DO NOT WEAR CHUCK TAYLORS! Hipsters recently learned that Chuck Taylors are the shoe choice of most non-conformists, and conforming to that stereotype is "soo over".*
- Buy an iPod. Its okay for Hipsters to support the man when it's Apple, Whole Foods or whatever major financial backer is *actually* behind their favorite indie publication.
- Research art galleries and shows in the area. This is a great first date with a hipster chick. Find the most disturbing art you can (trust me, if you live in any major metropolitan area, there's an artist that sculpts nude children out of dog shit...it's to protest the war). Plus, they serve wine and cheese at gallery openings. Hipster chicks love wine and cheese (never mind, now they hate it).
- Find a New York company that makes scarves that look like they're made for homeless people and a barber that's

blind. He'll give you the cut she's looking for. Then get some black glasses and a cardigan.
- Now get rid of your cardigan.
- Find a really obscure Middle Eastern brand of cigarettes. Don't smoke? Start smoking. This is important because hipster girls are like high schoolers and still think smoking is "cool". Also, it gives you something to do when you need to get out of a shitty concert.
- Find a good vintage store, because although you know the back story on your shoes and scarf, you don't care about your appearance man, it's whatevs.
- Drink PBR with a whiskey back because "you don't like mixed drinks"...I don't know why, no one does. Not even Chesterfield Nguyen.
- Ask Jeeves about existential philosophy. Scroll to "page 10" of the results and pick one of those guys to be your "favorite philosopher"...You HAVE to have a favorite philosopher. Now you can quote him when someone asks you if you want a PBR and say things like "Charles Finnigan-Mjumbo would say that *no one* actually wants a PBR dude" before you take it and slurp it down.
- Watch more Luke Wilson movies, but don't tell anyone because they're *way* too mainstream...just mimic his attitude.
- Find out who "The Maccabees" are.

Now you're ready, young Patiwan. Your Jedi training is complete...go out and get yourself a hipster girl...oh, but don't quote Star Wars...for some reason they don't like that.

- *Chapter Thirty* -

A Handsome Five Year Plan: Convincing the Girl at the Train Stop That I Have One

If you live in any type of urban center, chances are you take the bus or train to work. If not, stop being an idiot and start taking the bus or train to work.

Before you get all pissy and decide to go look at a generic poorly-drawn cartoon about how "it rains a lot in Seattle" or "Saracha is delicious ain't it?"...just know that I'm not lecturing you about your carbon footprint. I'm not telling you to do this because I'm an environmentalist...I'm telling you this because pretty, career-oriented girls who look all sexy in pencil skirts and tight blouses take the bus and/or train to work, and as a handsome man, it's your job to validate their decision to wear that skirt.

And isn't that where you'd rather be? Is that better than sitting in your Daewoo in twenty minutes of traffic for your three-mile drive, listening to the same song they played on the radio yesterday morning and thinking about the $250 a month you're paying for parking at your office? THERE ARE NO HOT GIRLS IN PENCIL SKIRTS IN YOUR DAEWOO!!!

But at the bus stop? There are plenty.

They're standing there with their iPods in, listening to something by *The Shins* while they sip their lattes and look all sexy in their 3-inch stilettos. Giggling at you as you sing along with "Poison" by Bel Biv DeVoe and mentally preparing for their first meeting of the day.

These broads are what you'd call "career-oriented"…They also don't like being called "broads" but that's neither here nor there.

In order to snag one of these girls, you're going to need to be just as career-oriented and driven as she is.

Haha, sorry, that was a type-o. What I meant to say was "In order to snag one of these girls, you're going to need to **trick her into thinking** that you're just as career-oriented and driven as she is.

And how do you do this? Well, I did some research (that's a lie, I don't research! I'm not even sure what I'm about to say in the next sentence…let's see what I pull out of my ass on this one shall we?) and I'd like to present to you the following aptly-named, overly-specific guide to convincing that sophisticated, professional young woman at your bus and/or train stop that you're as upwardly mobile as she is…and also that you know what "upwardly mobile" means:

THE OVERLY-SPECIFIC GUIDE TO CONVINCING THAT SOPHISTICATED, PROFESSIONAL YOUNG WOMAN AT YOUR BUS AND/OR TRAIN STOP THAT YOU'RE AS UPWARDLY MOBILE AS SHE IS…AND ALSO THAT YOU KNOW WHAT "UPWARDLY MOBILE" MEANS.

- **Look Busy:** Don't talk to her. That's creepy…and we'll get to it later. Instead, we're gonna make calculated moves to impress her without ever talking to her. WAY less creepy. You catch the bus at 6 AM every morning. There's no reason why you should be on the phone that early…unless you're talking to your Tokyo office or developers in Mumbai. And no…I may not have checked a time-zone map before I threw those examples out there…but I'm pretty sure they'll fly. If you're on the phone talking about your "mid-east production numbers" you'll look like you're involved in some high level stuff. *Pro-Tip: Make sure your phone is on silent, because there's nothing more embarrassing than pretending to be on a business phone call when your "Nothin but a G Thang" ringtone starts blasting.*
- **Go 'head an switch ya style up:** 50 Cent said that so it's GOTTA be true. If you first locked eyes with her while you were wearing a suit and tie, the next day, you should be wearing a pair of ripped jeans and a t-shirt. You gotta keep her on her toes. Was he interviewing yesterday? Does he work for some trendy tech start-up that has no dress code? No matter what she assumes, it'll imply success. Lock it in on the third day with some Docker's Flat Front Khakis. *Pro-Tip: You need one of those cool over-the-shoulder man purse bags that clearly has your laptop and a whole bunch of paperwork in it. If you wear a backpack with your jeans and t-shirt, she'll assume you had a presentation in Home Room the day before.*

- **Get a stylus:** Remember when PDAs and smart phones had those little pen-lookin things? Remember when "PDAs" were a thing? Do those even exist anymore? I don't care if your iPhone is touch screen. Nothing screams "I'm doing something important!" like a stylus. Pretend you're moving things around on your calendar and at one point say "dammit she double-booked me"...this implies that you're A. busy and B. important enough to have a secretary...sorry, I mean an "Administrative Assistant"....secretaries get all bitchy about that one.
- **All due respect to the good Doctor...but leave the "Beats By Dre" headphones at home:** Nothing says "I waste my money" like $300 headphones. Other things these headphones say are: "I'm on my way to the video arcade", "I love fads", "I'm probably listening to Solja Boi" and of course "I probably have a peanut butter and jelly sandwich in my airbrushed backpack"
- **Carry around a bunch of big rolled up pieces of paper:** sure, we live in a digital age where this isn't necessary. But nothing presents an image of someone successful and creative like implied blueprints or schematics. You probably have some old beer signs and Lil Kim posters in your room (what...doesn't everyone?), just roll those up back-side out (which oddly enough is Lil Kim's favorite position...thank you! I'm here all week). *Pro-Tip: The day you carry these, wear jeans with a shirt and tie...and some black-framed trendy glasses.*

The Payoff: If you can follow these simple steps, by the seventh day, she'll get so weak in the knees when she sees you that you'll have to catch her after she stumbles in her stilettos. Then you can say something super romantic like "Damn girl...you so fine I want to lick your kneecaps"

- *Chapter Thirty One* -

Finding Love: And by "Love" I mean "A Rich Girl"

You know what guys? Between student loans, rent, car payments, insurance, booze, hookers and blow (not to mention the subsequent funds for bail)...this life can get expensive for a handsome man! There's gotta be a better way to go about it.

Fiscal responsibility is clearly out of the question, so what other options do you have? The answer is simple: Just get yourself a sugar momma.

The "sugar daddy" concept is easy for women. Ask any lady: Where can you find rich guys? Answer: anywhere. There's always one around that you can seduce with your lady parts.

For guys, this becomes a bit trickier...especially in my hometown.

In Vegas, you go to industry night. In New York: it's hip to be broke. In LA: You're all douchebags anyway so no one cares. In Europe: You can't go outside without tripping and falling into a princess...but this is Seattle. Land of Internet Millionaires. You're EXPECTED to be rich. You can't just go to Bellevue because the rich girls there are *also* looking for a rich guy.

It's about time you had a resource to help you overcome this negative stereotype. Oh snap! I'm that resource!

First, you have to ask yourself an important question. You may not see it as a huge differentiator, but trust me, the personality types (not to mention what she'll be willing/able to do for your life) are two completely different things.

What are you looking for:

1. **A girl who has family money?** Short term Option: High yield for a quick ROI.
2. **A self-made, upwardly-mobile career woman?** Long term Option: This isn't the internet bubble. You're investing in bonds and saving for the long run. You'll make a healthy monthly profit off the interest, but the balloon payment comes later.

If you answered "A", then you should do one of the following:

- Get into sales. Sales is an easy place to look like you belong. Start playing golf and invite old, successful business guys out on the links (hint: if you call them "clients" it's a tax write off). One of them is bound to have a daughter. Schmooze him. Get in his good graces and lie about how you have a five-year plan and junk. Then find a way to meet his daughter. When you're with her? Pull out the "Fresh Prince" and switch to the bad boy routine. Rich chicks love that. This is the oldest trick in the book.

Point Value: 10 Dinners at El Gaucho, 42 bar tabs and your next electric bill paid. All prizes come with an expiration date.

- Go to a college library. And I don't mean a community college. Hell, you're aiming for the top so not even state schools fly here. Private school money only. Get a latte, find the oldest, biggest book you can and sit down next to her. Then you make contact. Then say something smooth like "I'm sorry, did you drop your *making out with a handsome man in the Law Book section* punch card?" If there's one thing a girl in the library loves, it's being hit on with a cheesy pick up line.

Point Value: An X-Box 360 and new TV for your apartment because she's sick of sleeping in the dorms.

- Crash private school reunions: She'll be looking to relive the glory days. Pretend you were an athlete or something. She'll eat it up. This option is good for two weeks, so you need to bring something else to the table during the process. This isn't difficult. "Once you've got the girl, any girl, you just have to give it to her right and then you can ask for anything. Groceries, drinks at the bar, car notes..." says one source who recently put his cable bill in a girl's name "In the words of The Mack: *Everything you throw at a broad will taste good if you're marinating that fish right.*"

Point Value: The hotel bill after the reunion…including ANYTHING you want from the mini-bar.

If you answered "B", then you should redirect your efforts here:

- Get arrested. Or better yet, get one of your buddies arrested. Then you can help him shop around for a lawyer. You don't care if she's good, because you didn't get arrested. You just care that she's hot. Lawyers will have some student loans to work with, but if you can wait those payments out, you're golden, ponyboy. Also: She's competitive. This keeps things interesting. Not that you're concerned with that.

Point Value: No more parking tickets! And a lifetime of anything you want from Pier 1.

- Go to the hospital. Doctors are there. And once you start dating, keep in mind that at the hospital, DOCTORS ARE THERE. She'll always be busy, and will just want you around when she's free. Haven't you seen "No Strings Attached"? You really should…Ashton is adorable.

Point Value: A new iPhone so you're always "on call" and a car so you can pick her up from 18-hour shifts (extra credit: this is easier if your car smells and sounds bad. She'll get embarrassed to ride with you).

- Start going to republican clubs/meetings. The girls are boring. And generally if they have politics that strong and that right-leaning…they'll be annoying as hell to listen to. On the upside, they're REALLY easy to piss off ("pro-choice" is the word you want to hang onto), and that's always funny.

Point Value: Some Playstation 3 games and a whole new wardrobe. Can't have you lookin' like a democrat son!

The "Catch-All" Answer:

If you're not particular, the best way to go **BY FAR** is the fundraiser.

At fundraisers, you'll get both types of money…I mean girl. Just make sure you don't get distracted by the cocktail waitresses. Focus on the bidders who aren't sitting with an old guy…

Point Value: These girls are always good for a week-long cruise through the Bahamas that she just "donated" 10k to The Catholic School System for.

I hope this has helped make you a better person and lead a more fulfilling life.

Disclaimer: This chapter is not advising any of you to take advantage of women in any way…just their credit cards.

- Chapter Thirty Two -

The Ten Things That Can Kill a Handsome Man's Game

The other day I got a text message from a girl that was simply a ;)

No words, no human interaction...Just a semicolon followed closely by a closed-parenthesis.

Now, I'm a good-lookin dude with SWEET calf muscles, so I understand why you would wink at me, but I'm also a charming, fun and witty conversationalist, and I expect words when you want to talk to me. I don't feel like that's too much to ask.

So I did what any self-respecting gentleman would do...I deleted her number and wrote a blog post about how stupid she was for doing that.

That blog post invoked about 40 winky-faced texts from various asshole friends, but also got some scathing responses from lady-folk who wanted me to know what a mistake I had just made.

"You know that was a booty call text, right?" inquired one girl who is welcome to send me a winky face anytime she'd like.

"I thought the winky face was a prequel to sexting?" replied another.

This went on all day. I got comments, emails and Facebook posts informing me that I'd "cock-blocked" myself by being over-critical.

I'm not a fan of the phrase "cock-block" because it's not a classy term. I don't mean it in a sexual way, but there aren't any synonyms in the thesaurus...so deal with it.

Now it's time to point out how awesome and unselfish I am: My first thought wasn't *"Damn I should track that girl down and call her for my own selfish benefit"*...No, I'm much more benevolent than that (which is my second best quality after my humility). My first thought was "I should write a chapter in my book about the worst types of cock blocks to a handsome man's game! That way these handsome dudes will know what to watch out for!"

CHAPTER ABOUT THE WORST TYPES OF COCKBLOCKS TO A HANDSOME MAN'S GAME

1. Yourself: It turns out that this is easier than you think. It's as simple as ignoring a winky face text. But it can also sneak up on you. You can be talking to a girl you just met, thinking *DAMN this chick is way into me!* And before you know it, you're complaining about your ex-girlfriend, talking about the difference between the time travel theories in *Back to the Future* and *Time Cop* or getting all nervous and twitchy and repeating the phrase "you're so pretty...you're just so pretty. I think I'm in love." No girl wants to hear that.

2. Girlfriends: I swear, every girlfriend I've ever had wants to keep me from flirting with the cute chick at the bar. It's BULLSHIT!

3. Girl's friends: Everyone's been victim to the "we gotta go girl" before. Her name is always *Suzie* or *Maggie* or something. She hates you and she hates fun. Her friends aren't allowed to be happy. She's too busy feeling miserable that no one's hitting on HER to allow you and her girl Stephanie to cuddle up in the back booth. All of a sudden she's telling Stephanie that you're a pervert and she's "pretty sure she saw you put something in her drink".

4. Sober friends: I've been this sober friend. You NEVER want to play wingman when you're the sober friend because drunk girls are the most annoying creatures that exist (although koalas are a close second. You might think they're cute but koalas are dicks...trust me). The point is this, sober guys: Sometimes in life, you have to put your own sanity aside for your friend. He needs this. He hasn't talked to a girl since Tina left him and he just found out she's engaged...Stupid Tina.

5. Drunk friends: The only thing worse than a sober friend is a drunk friend. You're having a nice wholesome conversation with a girl and all of a sudden she has a drink spilled all over her and is hearing about the time you guys got wasted in college and bought a goat that lived under your dorm room bed for a month. She wasn't ready for that story. NO ONE was.

6. Dragons: Be honest, have you EVER successfully hit on a chick when a dragon was around? No. They're a huge game-killer. Girls hate dragons. Always breathin' fire and tormenting villagers and stuff... Why do you think douchebags in Ed Hardy shirt always have dragons embroidered into their pants? That's not a "cool" look they're just assholes and don't want to see you happy.

7. Jax Teller: He rides a Harley and carries a giant knife. Jax Teller could steal almost anyone's wife or girlfriend. Just ask the Mayans. They know.

8. Bad Wingmen: Despite what you may think, this is different than your sober friend. The sober friend doesn't WANT to play wingman, but he's good at it. He's so indifferent that the girl he's entertaining will be all self-consciously intrigued. The bad wingman is the guy who can't play it cool. He says inappropriate things and makes this move about HIM. It wasn't about him. It was about you. Next time maybe your NEW best friend will get it right.

9. STDs: Nothing kills a vibe more than a girl saying "Hey, I have syphilis...and not a calm, normal kind. The kind that killed Al Capone."

10. Other guys: Stupid other guys. They're ALWAYS trying to talk to the same girl you are. Can't they just get their own? Other guys are my least favorite people in the world. Girls LOVE other guys because other guys will buy them drinks and lie to them: Lies and free drinks are a pretty girl's kryptonite.

Knowledge is power you guys. It's up to you to notice these signs and counteract the cockblock. Get your secondary involved. Send a cock-linebacker in to distract the cockblocker so you can cocktackle that quarterback and...uh...okay I kind of lost my train of thought and might have ruined football for myself. I'm gonna go play Madden and try to forget about this.

- *Chapter Thirty Three* -

Cooking with a Handsome Man: A Recipe for Love...or at Least a Sweet Hickey

You've ALL heard the old adage: *A woman's place is barefoot in the kitchen...*

What they *don't* tell you is that's because it would be silly for her to put on clothes when she comes out to taste the delicious hollandaise sauce you've made for breakfast-in-bed. HI-YO! No but seriously let me know if you want the recipe...it's like heaven got boiled down to a creamy froth.

Regular Fellas: do you cook for your lady? You should.

Single Fellas: do you cook for the girl you want to be your lady? You should.

And that's what we're going to focus on today because cooking for a girlfriend isn't a big deal. You should be doing half the cooking anyway because of…you know…ummm… "empowerment" or something. I forgot to pay attention in the 90s but I'm pretty sure this is what they were whining about.

How to butter her bread on the first date, and NOT EVEN IN A DIRTY WAY!

Cooking on a first date is 98.7% fool-proof (which isn't an accurate stat, but it's 100% true). It's a win-win situation! You don't even have to be good at it!

1. If you're bad at cooking, then you look adorable and "so sweet" for trying and then you *never have to cook for her again* because your food was awful and your use of fish sauce made that coconut chicken taste like kitten piss!
2. If you're good at cooking, you will wind up in a Jacuzzi with a bottle of prosecco as Al Greene (or whoever your favorite sexy musician is, although if it's not Al Greene, you're wrong) serenades you and your lady while you point at stars or something like that.

If she's *not* impressed that you're cooking for her on the first date, then you should stop caring what she thinks because she doesn't have a soul. She probably hates toys and Star Wars and fun anyway so you should move on to someone better.

So don't waste this cookbook on her.

Waste it on that other 98.7% of women who like food and handsome gentlemen cooking it for them as they playfully banter back and forth about who's better-looking (pretend to give in because *clearly* she's gorgeous…it's okay, we know the truth).

Sautéed and Basted: Tips For Cooking on The First Date

- **Use Cooking Terms:** This is super important. Not because you want to seem "knowledgeable" or "intelligent" or anything that trivial (my Spell Check just auto-corrected both "knowledgeable" and "intelligent" for me...that's depressing). No, you want to use cooking terms because subconsciously, we all think of cooking terms in a sexy, sensual way. Don't believe me? Do me a favor: Watch the Food network for 15-minutes this afternoon and *repeat* everything you hear in a seductive tone. "I'll simmer that sauce on low until it gets all creamy and thick" or "You want to baste the turkey every 20-minutes so it stays juicy and moist"...With the exception of "moist", those are all really sensual words that will have her thinking "Dang this stud really knows his way around a kitchen" but she'll be using "kitchen" as a euphemism.
- **Tiny Bowls:** You know how your mom always had those tiny little bowls around that looked like they could only fit one mini-wheat in them? Did you ever wonder what they were for? They're for looking like you know what you're doing. Before she comes over, measure out all the spices you plan on using and put them in these bowls. This way, you can just casually toss them in your pot or pan or wok or whatever you're using while you talk about the current economic climate of the Euro-zone. **Pro-Tip:** *Cooking something that won't require a lot of spices? Just add stuff! Use ones like "Tarragon" or "Paprika" or anything you've never seen in an actual recipe. These aren't real things. They're fake spices that chefs invented in the 13th century to look like they're doing something complicated. That way the king couldn't have them killed. These spices have no flavor so you can add them to anything.*

- **No Seafood!** Trust me. You don't want to cook seafood on the first date. This isn't *Hitch*. You don't want an allergic reaction that has her doubled over a toilet all night to be her first impression of you...Save that for a fourth date when you're kind of sick of her and are looking for a way out.
- **Vegetables:** You *have* to cook with vegetables. Girls like vegetables. Apparently Macaroni and Cheese with some hotdogs cut up in it doesn't fly on a first date...You have to add some frozen peas or something. But if you're cooking a grown-up meal, you should have vine-ripened tomatoes and cilantro and junk. That way you can chop the cilantro as she's sitting there, and you can do that smooth thing where you throw the towel over your shoulder. You might think this is only okay if you're a bartender...but it's not. Anyone can do it. Just try not to cut your fingers off because I've heard that's No. 3 on the "Least Sexy Things to Do on a Date" list (right behind: "picking your nose" and "making out with her grandpa in an ihop bathroom").
- **Candles:** Light some candles. Girls dig ambiance. As far as I can tell, "ambiance" means "candles". Don't have any candles? Here's a trick: They sell them at almost *every* store! I had no idea. You can just buy candles everywhere. Once your candles are lit, you should play music that has an acoustic guitar in it. Acoustic guitars and ambiance go hand-in-hand.
- **Add wine:** No, I'm not telling you to get her drunk...get your life together, that's creepy. I'm telling you to add wine to whatever you're cooking. If you open a bottle and splash some wine into your saucepan, you're gonna look super legit. Just try not to splash any on your pants...that stuff is hard to get out.
- **Presentation:** Broads love presentation. Have a serving dish and stuff. I know, I know...as a guy, this makes NO sense. It's an extra dish to wash and an extra step before

this delicious Lamb Rangoon can be in my mouth! But you've gotta do it...You're talking about the girl who got her hair did, make-up just right and came straight there from a mani-pedi JUST for dinner. Just make her help with the extra dishes. Then you can spray her with that hose thing and before you know it, everyone's clothes are too wet to keep on!

I hope these cooking tips help! If you follow these simple instructions, you should be in the Jacuzzi in no time. Enjoy the meal my handsome friends.

- Chapter Thirty Four -

If You're Over 25, There Are Only 10 Girls Left

I wish I got married young.

Haha, that's silly. I'm just kidding.

But that being said, I really hate guys who say that they "can't imagine being married. It'd be SOO monotonous bro!"

Yup...those are also the types of guys who always call you "bro".

If you're over 25 and are complaining about how "monotonous" marriage would be, then you're not paying attention to the monotony your own life.

And no, I'm not talking about the chicken breast and brown rice you have for dinner every night...Sriracha never gets old.

What I'm talking about is your dating life.

You may not be aware of this yet, but you get to a point in your late 20s when you realize that there are only a few types of un-married women out there...and at this point you're probably just cycling through them and trying to convince yourself that each one is special and unique.

As soon as you start to recognize these stereotypical and disrespectful labels, you can begin categorizing the women you date and lose all hope of ever developing a relationship with any of them.

I'm not trying to depress you, so I apologize if this is hard to read, but a handsome man doesn't hide from the truth: He faces it head-on.

THE TEN TYPES OF WOMEN OVER 25

1. Bitter alcoholics in the making: It starts so innocent. She's just a big fan of happy hour, that's all! That's her thing! So what if she's got plans every night of the week? So what if when you go to her apartment she's already on her second bottle of wine...at noon. It's not a big deal because she's all smiles...right now anyway. But that's because she's too drunk to remember the fact that she got hammered and hit on her boss's husband at last year's Christmas party...give her that few rare hours of sobriety that she experiences weekdays before lunch...She'll get there.

2. Single moms/Teachers: These two get grouped into the same category because they both have children they're close to, but you never have to see. After spending time with these consistently drunk, co-dependent, morally flexible women, your first thought is always "who the hell lets these crazy broads around children???" But it's cool. They're happy to pretend that they love the "no-strings-attached" thing…and they always have Capri Sun.

3. The "I'm married to my job" girls: These girls are usually boring…but they're boring in a variety of ways. Either they hate popular culture and shun every aspect of it, or they feel like their job is making them grow up too fast so they cling to youth by watching *American Idol, Jersey Shore* or *Millionaire Matchmaker*. Face it, you date her because she wears business suits and looks like a naughty librarian and once let you play CEO and secretary at her office on a Saturday…but after that novelty wears off, she's just another chick who wants you to throw away your WWE championship belt autographed by Ted DiBiase and get a job. But SCREW that! Put her in The Million Dollar Dream!

4. "Daddy's my best friend" (read: rich girls): Her worldview is so slanted that she might be way into you from the start…but only because she doesn't understand math or realize that you can't provide the life she's accustomed to. She's never paid a bill in her life, so she doesn't factor that into her decision to date you, which is sweet…until you make the mistake of buying a necklace from Macy's instead of Cartier because you're a struggling sports writer and she flips out and complains that "you don't love her enough to buy her nice things" in that pouty, whiny voice and all of her friends take her side BUT THAT'S ONLY BECAUSE YOUR DADDY FLIES THEM TO VAIL EVERY YEAR IN HIS PRIVATE JET, ALLISON! uhh…Sorry that got a little personal.

5. Skanks: You can tell yourself all you want that she hooked up with you in the bathroom stall of that nightclub because "you had a real connection"…but you know as well as I do that she was the first girl to go to third base in 6th grade, the cheerleader getting spirit-fingered by the entire offensive line in high school, and the frat house favorite in college. You need to take a deep breath and remember what Doctor Dre said: You can't make a ho a housewife.

6. Hipster girls: She hates that you have a real job and corporate ambition...but hey, someone's gotta pay for those feathers in her hair and PBR tallboys.

7. The "I'm one of the guys" girls: She seems cool because she can hang, but did you think about how that's gonna turn out a year or two down the road? When "hanging with the guys" is something you'll want to do to get AWAY from her? The benefit of girls not liking sports as much as you do is that you can say "Hey I'm gonna go watch Australian Rules Football" and she'll have NO interest in following you.

8. The "I'm afraid of dying alone" girls: Let me ask you a question...how many cats does she have? If the answer is "more than zero" then she's already told her mom about you...and not in a "oh girl, he's so hot" because her mom is her best friend kind of way, but in a "can you clear an extra space at the dinner table for Thanksgiving?" kind of way.

9. Gold diggers: Obviously she's not very good at it because she's still single. Give her a dollar and tell her to get a new game plan because this one's not working.

10. Girls you SHOULD date because you have everything in common, but won't because you're busy getting down with 1-9: You've got this friend. You don't know it, because you look at her like one of the guys, but don't worry...some other dude sees her breasts. He'll lock it down soon.

- *Chapter Thirty Five* -

Facebook Flirting: The New "Drunken Make-Out in a Bar Full of Your Girlfriend's Friends"

Look, you don't want to be "that guy" who makes all of his mistakes public. A handsome man makes his mistakes behind closed doors and bottles them up forever.

> **InnocentGirl** Just got my bathing suits for the summer!
> 12 hours ago · Comment · Like
>
>> **NotInnocentResponse** I want to touch you in the bathing suit area and oh crap I'm just now realizing that everyone and their grandma can read this nevermind
>> 11 hours ago

Allow me to paint you a picture: In college, I had a friend. This friend had a girlfriend. This friend was a "bad person" and he liked to "cheat on this girlfriend."

Wait...I'm sorry guys; those quotes didn't belong there because it made it sound like I was being ironic. I was not. He liked to have sex with girls who were not his girlfriend.

This friend's dilemma? All of his girlfriend's friends went to our school. So one night we were at a party, and he was having a polite conversation with a young lady. This polite, mild-mannered conversation progressed delicately into sloppy, drunk, ass-grabby making out.

Enter the girlfriend's friend: This girl called his girlfriend, who called him and yelled for hours. Then Suzie Whistleblower told the girl that he had been politely molesting that he had a girlfriend, and thus ended that encounter. It was very entertaining as a spectator.

Sigh...times were so simple then, weren't they? You know, before "the internet". And when I say "the internet" I mean "Facebook"...Myspace doesn't count. Why not? Because you had to *approve* things people said to/about you. Facebook is the freakin wild west of sloppy drunken mistakes.

Sloppy Drunken Facebook

Now I've never been caught in either scenario because this all requires too much effort...so I had to do some research. And while I was doing this research, I got super bored...then I started watching Youtube videos. Then I got a text message and got distracted playing Angry Birds on my phone. Then I made up some statistics. Here they are:

1. **78% of modern hook-ups between people over 23 started with flirting on facebook.**
2. **47% of modern break-ups between people over 27 started when one party caught the other flirting with some little tart on facebook.**

3. **Monkeys having sex with other monkey is a key factor in 87% of the world's monkey population.**

Crazy right? I didn't know monkeys liked doin it so much! But also, nothing I just said is true. That's the problem with the internet, *just because something's here, doesn't make it real*. People have accepted this, and so "Facebook flirting" doesn't seem real. This is a direct corollary to the "sorority girl logic":

Sorority Girl Logic: If I was too drunk to *remember* blowing that guy in the bathroom of an Arbys because his backwards Abercrombie and Fitch hat was frayed and I thought it made him look cute, it didn't happen.

Same thing when it comes to joking about hooking up with one of your Facebook friends. It all starts out friendly and cool, but before you know it, someone else can see the post:

> **DumbGirl** Going out for shots with the girls tonight WOOOO lol OMG!
> 10 hours ago · Comment · Like
>
> **StupidGuywithGirlfriend** Haha, who's bed are YOU waking up in tomorrow?
> 9 hours ago
>
> **DumbGirl** OMG Yours silly!
> 8 hours ago
>
> **StupidGuywithGirlfriend** Haha well don't tempt me with a good time!
> 7 hours ago
>
> **DumbGirl** I'm totally texting you right now. You HAVE to come meet up ;)
> 7 hours ago
>
> **StupidGuywithGirlfriend** Oh I'm there!
> 7 hours ago
>
> **Girlfriend'sFriendWhoKnowsBothOfThem** Ummmm....I'm telling Tina you fucking scumbag!
> 6 hours ago

This is when you get in trouble. It all seemed so INNOCENT at first. Now you have to dig your way out of this situation and explain how "those pics were from WAY before you and Stacey (it's always a Stacey) ever met:

> **StupidGuy** Baby I'm so sorry. Please answer my calls. It wasn't what it looked like.
> 11 hours ago · Comment · Like
>
> **JadedGirlfriend** Whatever! Get the hell out of my life!
> 10 hours ago
>
> **StupidGuy** She's just my friend! We were just joking around. You know you're my babygirl!
> 9 hours ago
>
> **JadedGirlfriend** So what...you got that bitch PREGNANT through facebook??? Yeah...I just talked to her you ASSHOLE!!!
> 9 hours ago
>
> **StupidGuy** ...shit
> 8 hours ago

And then you wind up in the ever famous **"Facebook Break up"** which is mad entertaining for the rest of us, but will probably suck for you.

My advice? Don't ever bring emotions or love into the internet world. Leave it to sports stats, kitten videos and porn like the Good Lord intended.

- Chapter Thirty Six -

"Let's Watch a Movie" and Other Ways Girls Tell Handsome Men to Take Their Pants Off

I sometimes forget how awesome I am...But then I have weeks like this one.

Example: I smiled at the coffee girl and got a free drink. I'm growing out a beard so there's even MORE manliness exuding from my pores (which are invisible because my complexion is magnificent).

Better Example: my flat-front, iron-free Dockers made two women at the bus-stop brace themselves to keep from fainting.

It's been a good week...for me. Not everyone has been so lucky. My friend Adam's week has NOT been like my Dockers: **He had a few wrinkles.**

Last night, we were hanging out, getting some happy hour eats with a few female friends, and one of them made a comment that Adam and I "are too easily distracted."

I enjoy talking about what women think is wrong with me, so naturally I turned to Adam and said "Wow that's interesting...so who would win in a fight; A ghost or a grizzly bear? BUT the ghost is the ghost of Val Kilmer."

The girls kept talking, and mentioned that they were going to head out. One of them turned to Adam and said "Do you want to come check out my new TV? It's pretty awesome!"

And Adam, who has been interested in Shmarci for years, said "No that's cool I'm gonna hang out with Kev for a while. Kevin are we talking fat Val Kilmer? Or Val Kilmer back when he was *Iceman*?"

After the girls left, I slapped Adam on the back of the hand like he was a small child. How could he miss such an obvious sign???

That's when I realized: Adam's a guy. We're distracted by Val Kilmer and we miss the signs that women throw at us. Well...you do anyway:

MISSING THE SIGNS: She's throwin curveballs that you're not ready for

1. Lets watch a movie: I don't know if you know this, but girls don't watch movies. It's true. Once a year, they'll check out the new *Sex and The City* or whatever crap Kate Hudson is putting out, but other than that, they use movies as their siren song to lure you into their bed. "Lets watch a movie" really means "Lets put a DVD in and make it to the main menu, where that 4-second snippet of soundtrack will play on repeat for hours while I take advantage of you in a variety of exciting ways."

2. Can you come fix/move/lift something for me: She doesn't really need help moving her bed from one side of the room to the other…it has wheels. What she NEEDS is to "accidentally" stumble into you while you're moving it so you both fall playfully onto the bed. **Hint:** She doesn't usually redecorate with candles lit and Jodeci's *Forever My Lady* playing in the background.

3. Let me cook dinner: Girls cook dinner for one reason…to get you alone in their apartment. You know this is true because that's the same reason you cook dinner for *them*. If they just wanted to enjoy your company and NOT serve you dessert out of their belly button, they would have just asked you out to a restaurant. That way they'd eat for free.

4. Come play Scrabble: What, did you think she *actually* wanted to play Scrabble? Of course not! We have *Words With Friends* and you could have done that remotely. She wanted you sitting across from her on the couch staring into her eyes while she pretends to get upset that you played "Qi", giving her the opportunity to lunge at you across the game board spilling your wine and forcing you both to take your shirts off. On an unrelated note, has anyone ever played Strip-Scrabble? Would that make it less boring?

5. Come drink this great bottle of wine with me: Right…because you're a huge wine connoisseur. You know all about the difference between a fine Chilean Malbec and a 7-Eleven bottle of *Arbor Mist*. Here's a hint: neither does she. She just likes to feel classy. That's why she didn't say "come over, get smashed and do me."

6. Come listen to music: Have you ever gone to "listen to music" at a girls house and had her blast a Solja Boi song? No. But you have gone over to play Scrabble and drink a bottle of wine and had her throw on a William Bell or Raphael Saadiq album. *Side Note: If you don't know who either of those guys are, you're not doing life right. Be better. Your lady friend deserves more.*

7. I'm all wet can I come in: Anytime she says something that sounds like it should be in a low-rent porno, she's interested. Also, she may or may not use that opportunity to rob you because really…who talks like that? This isn't Vegas.

- Chapter Thirty Seven -

You Want a "Good Girl" and She Wants a "Nice Guy"

Yesterday, a friend who was feeling a little down after a recent break-up asked me, "Where do you meet good girls these days?"

This is an interesting question, so in order to try to help him better, I asked "Ewwww! Why would you want a good girl?"

To which he responded, "Kevin, I don't know how you do it. Where do you meet all these super sexy girls that throw themselves at you and NONE of them are bar skanks? I'm sick of the crazy bar chicks I meet all the time and I want to be more awesome and cool like you! Also, and this has nothing to do with anything, but dammit Kevin you make me feel like less of a man!"

This brings about an interesting point that you can all benefit from: When you talk to me and are saying boring things, I hear something completely different in my head. This ability (it *is so* an ability!) has come in handy with every girl I've ever dated:

Girl: Kevin do you ever think about our future together? I want eight babies and a house in the suburbs with curtains and area rugs.

Kevin: That's a great question girlfriend. And yes...I DO think Wolverine vs. Optimus Prime would be an epic fight.

But also, you should know that there are TONS of places to meet people other than bars. Ladies, this applies to you as well (but you know, only so I can make sexist jokes, the rest of it is for the handsome men).

Here are a few places to meet people, coupled with advice and warnings for each (use at your own discretion. I accept no responsibility for the outcome...you're not as handsome as me so these options may fail miserably):

The Bookstore

Fellas: this is a good place to try because girls who go there are only interested in *looking* like they read. Trust me: The girls who just like reading are at home with their Kindle and eight cats crying into their "Sleepy Time Tea" about why more guys aren't like Rhett from*Gone With the Wind.*

Warning: stay away from the "Twilight" section. Those girls are hoes...or vampires. Either way it can't be good.

Ladies: This is a safe bet for the same "Kindle" reason: You know that the guy buying a book is probably buying it as a present...which means he'll probably buy you presents if you show him your lady parts.

Warning(s): This holds the same principle as meeting a guy in Victoria's Secret: It's possible he's buying that book for another chick. Also, avoid the "poetry" section because no one wants a boyfriend they can beat up.

Coffee Shop

Fellas: This is a good place to meet that hipster girl you're trying to go for. Wear a scarf or a shirt that has a picture of Che Guevara on it or something. She'll dig it.

Pro Tip: Don't order a "black coffee". I did this the other day and you'd have thought I'd summoned the ghost of Hitler. "Ummmm, we only serve AMERICANOS here." And by the way, as far as I could tell, "Americano" means BLACK COFFEE!

Ladies: This is a good place to meet a guy because you can scout him out. Is he the one with the face tattoo and Mohawk or is he the one with the trendy skinny tie and macbook sitting by the fire with his tri latte?

Pro Tip: Be careful not to wind up with "Extra hot Grande Mochachino with no whip no foam and just a dash of cinnamon" guy...he's got issues.

Grocery Store

Fellas: The grocery store is the "eharmony.com" of real life. Where else can you find someone who has their life choices laid out in front of you? "OMG! You like Cinnamon Toast Crunch but opt for the Malt-o-Meal version and plan on eating a single chicken breast for dinner TOO???"

Warning: Despite our need as a culture to avoid stereotypes, there's still a 96% chance she's married. Pay close attention to the cart.

Ladies: Same concept. You can find out a lot about someone by what he puts in his cart. If he has a cart full of vegetables and bread and meat and...other grown up stuff...he's probably married. If he has a cart full of frozen pizzas, he's probably single.

Warning: If he has a cart full of Kool-Aid, you're probably racist for assuming I was about to make a black joke.

The Gym

Fellas: This is a tricky situation, because you automatically come across as a douche, but at the same time, she's at the gym *hoping* someone notices her.

Warning: You need to put in time on this one. You can't just walk into a gym for the first time and start hitting on girls. The upside to this is that the extra time there will give you some SWEET calf muscles.

Ladies: This is also tough. Lots of guys go to the gym, but without their collared shirts and gel in their hair, it's hard to tell which ones own jeans embroidered with dragons.

Warning: You have a 90% chance of finding a douchebag, because they're the ones going to the gym to talk to chicks.

I hope this helps you find your so-called "good girl" or "nice guy" but chances are, they're going to murder you in your sleep anyway...what, too far?

- *Chapter Thirty Eight* -

How to Get Out of the Friend Zone: Stop Being Her Friend, Dummy!

Imagine if you will: Adam and Stacey. Two people that have formed a *special*connection. Adam's feelings have grown stronger by the day, and he feels it's time to make his move.

So Adam tries to kiss and/or touch Stacey's boobie (not kiss her boobie, that would be creepy in most settings). Stacey pulls back...and after a long awkard pause...she drops this bomb:

"*Look Adam...I just don't see you that way. You're like one of my **best friends**now and I wouldn't **EVER** want to do anything to jeopordize that.*"

Oh snap! Adam just got his ass *friend zoned*. We've all been there haven't we?

Friend Zone (fr-e-nd z-o-n) n.: A state of being in which a male who had been pursuing the act of copulation with a female is no longer seen as a viable sexual partner for the aforementioned female.

The friend zone is a tricky spot you guys. In order to get out of it, you have to understand how you got there in the first place, and I can't help you do that by mincing words so I'm going to be honest: you messed up son. What were you waiting for? She wanted you when you first met but you're the man, and despite any illusion she tries to paint about "gender equality"...she *still wants you to be the man.*

My guess is it went a little like this: You met. She was into you. You were into her. You hung out. She thought you were just being a gentleman and being polite by not inviting her into the dirty bathroom of the seedy bar to make out and then go back to your dumpy apartment to wake up the neighbors because you're too cheap to buy a bed that doesn't sound like you're stepping on a cat everytime you use it. So you went out for coffee instead. It was nice.

And that's about it...as soon as she told her friends "it was nice", you were in the friend zone. So now what? You go to museums and concerts and eat hot dogs in the park and basically all the boring parts of being a boyfriend. Oh, and she complains to you about the asshole that she's dating, all the while you're thinking *I could have been that asshole.*

So let's test your metal my friend. Is it possible? Do you dare...

How to Get Out of the Friend Zone

There are a few ways to do this, and I gotta tell you...you might not like any of them (don't worry, I don't mean "whip it out on the couch" or anything gross like that...this method only has a 16% closing ratio in *normal* circumstances).

- **Date one of her friends.** She can't get mad, because you're in the friend zone; it's practically *her duty* to set you up. This has two levels to it: 1. She gets to test the waters. "Would he be a good boyfriend? Seems like he is with Christy. Did I make a mistake?" and 2. Women are terrible friends! She'll want you just because her friend has you *and she doesn't*! You're like a grownup version of the Barbie Dream house.
- **If you can't date one of her friends; date anyone.** Just find a girl who will come around a lot and talk about how *amazing* you are. It's a bonus if she brings up how awesome you are in the bedroom. If you suck in that department, get a female friend to lie and pretend she's your girlfriend who you're givin' it to on the regs. Trust me, she'll do it: women love lying and being involved in complicated schemes that hurt other women.
- **Flip it on her:** Make sure she knows she's "just one of the guys". This may sound tough, but ignore her breasts and act grossed out when she talks about other guys like she's a gay guy talking about how much ass they get. But on the flipside, talk casually about dates of your own. Also, invite her to sports stuff. This will make her feel uncomfortable and it should be your constant goal to keep her in a state of limbo.
- **Don't go to her yoga class with her:** Stop doing the "gay friend" activities. She probably has a gay friend who's role you're stealing. Quit being that guy. She's never slept with him.
- **If you really have trouble coming across as an asshole: Drop the "L Word"**. Say things like "You're the only one who actually knows me" and other things you saw in a John Cusack movie. This works if you actually mean it...Wait, sorry, this works if you actually

mean it *or* if you have a quick get-away plan for the next morning and can skip out of her apartment clicking your heels together and singing Justin Timberlake's hit song "What goes around".

Use this information wisely my friends. This is not meant to be used to "scam" girls because honestly...these broads will fall for anything.

- Chapter Thirty Nine -

The Game of Love: Check the Scoreboard

There's a really trendy hipster coffee shop down the block from me. It's one of those places where everyone is wearing two scarves and you expect them all to be either an ideological communist or play the bongos in a bluegrass/reggae crossover band.

I was in there the other day doing what every d-bag in a coffee shop does: pretending I'm a writer...and this girl walked in.

I didn't pay much attention at first because I was too busy furrowing my brow trying to look like I was working on something important while sipping my iced venti non-fat latte (don't judge me, they're delicious and I went to a monster truck and coal-mining convention afterword to make up for it).

But back to the girl. She was standing in line behind an uber-hipster. One of those guys that's too cool for clothes that fit and had a disturbing amount of "middrift" showing. As he walked away with his tiny cup of something I can't pronounce, this cute girl turns back to the barista and says "He's sorry he had to go…he left his dignity at home."

Do you hear that Gilmore Girl level wit? She came up with that on the fly! Like a Scott Pilgrim character without blue hair and roller skates!

She gets a point!

You see, I also learned a little something I didn't know about dating this weekend: It involves a point system now. And yes…I was super excited when I found this out.

How do I know this? My sister-in-law's best friend apparently had my brother on a point system when she first met him.

Naturally, as he IS my brother and shares my charming, witty and handsome gene pool (ours is an infinity pool with a diving board and one of those twisty waterslides)…he nailed the "point" test.

As a lifestyle blogger – which is what someone called me on Twitter the other day (it made me feel a little dirty for some reason…Probably because I don't know what it means) – I like this "point-system" idea. As a guy who invariably dates girls that have insane tendencies…I really like this idea. But as a sports fan? I LOVE this idea.

So I figured, why can't I make one of my own? I sat down and got to work on a Handsome Man's point system. I gotta tell you, it was a lot harder than I expected it to be. But now that the list is in place, I've gotta roll with it. I'm only dating girls who pass the test. You can do it too. I've built the test for you.

The Handsome Man's Dating Point System

Wait...does that sound sexist and superficial like I'm judging women on an arbitrary set of standards that have no real bearing on a person's character? Yes? Okay good that's what I was going for.

THE HANDSOME MAN'S SEXIST AND SUPERFICIAL POINT SYSTEM BASED ON AN ARBITRARY SET OF STANDARDS

- If she's ever dated a guy named Brad longer than it took for him to tell her his name was "Brad": **Subtract one point.**
- If she can name the player who hit the "Shot Heard Round The World" in the 1951 National League Pennant Race: **Add one point.**
- If she actually enjoyed the movie *The Kids Are Alright:* **Subtract one point.**
- If she owns a wiffle ball bat: **Add one point**...if that wiffle ball bat has a crack down the seam from excessive use: **Add two points.**
- If she "just doesn't get why people liked Michael Jackson": **Subtract one point.**
- If she will engage in a heated debate about whether or not the Rebel Alliance truly defeated the Empire: **Add one point.**
- If she calls "just to talk" more than once a day: **Subtract one point.**
- If she owns a Green Lantern t-shirt that isn't ironic: **Add one point.**
- If she got offended by the "just to talk" point: **Subtract one point.**

- If she doesn't laugh, and even better *respects* your hetero-crush on The Rock: **Add one point.**
- If she loves Katherine Heigel and/or Grey's Anatomy: **Subtract one point.**
- If she points out a ridiculously hot girl, just in case you missed it: **Add one point.**
- If she ask "what are you thinking about" and then doesn't believe you when you say "Sandwiches": **Subtract one point.**
- If she complements you....I know I know, this one's not funny but hell, a guy likes to hear he's pretty every once and a while: **Add one point.**
- If she has an opinion about Twilight that *ISN'T* "they fuckin sparkle! I'll take Blade any day": **Subtract one point.**
- If she sends you pics of her kissing the camera with the caption "missing you"....I know it's cutesy and lame but what am I made of stone? That's adorable: **Add one point.**

And you're finished! Congrats! Now lets tally up your total. I'll give you a moment to go back because you're clearly not very bright...I mean, you've read forty chapters of this book already:

Scoring Guide:

Less than zero: For the last time stop hitting on high school girls! It's getting creepy.

1-4 Points: Give her a shot! Oh, but uh...strongly weigh her looks because that *may* be all you're stuck with.

5-8 Points: If she scores this high, be prepared to meet the d-bag she's dating who's doesn't appreciate at her at all...fate you cruel cruel bitch!

9-10 Points: Do me a favor and take a picture of the unicorn she's riding…because she doesn't exist.

It's a tough world out there. And I hope this helps you find the girl of your dreams…or at least ensure that you never have to watch Grey's Anatomy.

So now that I've sufficiently helped you to find and impress the girl you've been looking for, we should probably equip you a little bit for what you're in for once you start dating. This next section will provide a start, but don't you worry, I'll give you a sequel eventually.

Part IV

Relationships Are About Winning

- *Chapter Forty* -

A Handsome Man's Guide to Dating Co-workers...Dating Them Good and Hard

Look at *[insert hot female coworker]*...sittin over there in their cubicle being all pretty and stuff. I'm trying to work dammit, *where does she get off???*

That was you. You said that. Probably this morning. It's tough working with a total hottie right?

Workplace romance: The oldest riddle known to man. Human beings have been struggling with this since Jesus:

John 13:21: And Jesus doth spake unto Peter, "I know we work together so this is mass inappropriate, but did you see Mary Magdalene's new frock bro?"

And we still struggle with these questions today. Is it a good idea? Is it worth the risk? Would anyone notice an "out of order" sign and wild animal noises coming from the copy room for the next three hours?

The point is, how do you know if you should go after that hot chick in accounting? And guess what...I'm here to help:

How you know if you should go after that hot chick in accounting:

The simple answer: Probably not...But this isn't a simple world. I can safely say as someone who has successfully had several unsuccessful relationships with coworkers...sometimes it's totally boss.

Side Note: I'm thinking about bringin back "boss"...thoughts?

There are a lot of "pros" to dating within the office:

- You could get caught, which makes it *super* sexy.
- Sometimes it's not even allowed, which makes it *super* even-sexier.
- It's convenient: she is always around when you're the most bored (less sexy, but still awesome).
- Pencil skirts (sexiest).

There's pretty much only one "con" in this situation:

- She could turn out to be crazy and hold your paycheck because 90% of the time the girl you're messing with works in HR and now you're broke and have this girl stalking you outside your window all night and telling your fellow co-workers about your "intimacy issues" and fear of clowns all day.

Now that we've weighed the pros and cons, I'm going to assume you weren't paying attention and have decided to proceed with the "wooing" period. If you don't know what "wooing" is, it's probably because you're under the age of 45 and will refer to this as the "I'm bout to holla at this trick" period.

There are things you need to know before you begin your workplace courtship. Here they are:

- Be aware of the **"office hot vs. real hot"** paradox. He/she looks better than they actually are because you're bored. Also, next to a spreadsheet, ANYONE looks good. "She's only hot because she's skinny and semi-cute," says Tim Bowman, who watches a lot of porn. "You're probably like *Not true, Gina in my office is smokin' hot!* And you're wrong, Gina is a bitch and stop saying *smokin'* you tool. Everyone knows pretty girls don't have to work." **Pro Tip: Go out for coffee in a very public place, this will give you a more effective barometer.**
- Don't tell your other co-workers once you start dating. It's more fun when it's a secret. Once people know about it, it's like a real relationship and who wants one of those? **Disclaimer: It really doesn't matter what you do to prevent it; eventually she'll tell everyone.**
- Take advantage of office Christmas parties. The Christmas party is the "get out of jail free" card with co-workers. Everyone already plans on blaming their actions on alcohol. Trust me; the girl who's been checking out your sweet calf muscles in the elevator has been thinking about the things she wants to do to you at that party *for months*. **Warning: Beware of the girl who doesn't usually wear librarian glasses but has them at the party. Her plan involves handcuffs.**

- Ladies: Cosmo says to "test the waters". Apparently, you can tell if a coworker wants to sleep with you by how much time he spends hanging around your cubicle. Please Cosmo...*In this economy?* This isn't the 80s. I'm not trying to lose my job and get sued for sexual harassment. Plus: ignoring broads works *way* better because she starts thinking "why isn't he talking to me? I'm a pretty girl!" **Bonus Points: This also helps you weed out the "office hot" coworkers.**
- Ladies: I haven't given you any advice in a while, and I know I said this book was for you too. Sorry, here's one for you: Don't date married guys...unless they're rich. You're welcome.

Hopefully this helps you. Chances are it won't and you'll still end up making the same mistakes we all do, but screw it, what else are you gonna do with that eight hours a day? WORK???

- *Chapter Forty One* -

Your Girlfriend Wants to "Fix" You…A Handsome Man Would Let Her

I wear cardigan sweaters. Argyle ones. There…I said it. That felt good.

Why did I feel that was important to tell you? I'll get to that.

Oh! Also important: Sometimes, in the winter, I rock a scarf and a trendy pea coat. I have a decorative globe next to an artsy photograph on my bookshelf that's full of books I've *actually read*. I even do my laundry once a week, fix my bed every morning and shower regularly.

Sure, I'd still rather play football than hold your purse while you shop, and I may or may not be watching cartoons as I write this, but all-in-all, one thing is becoming clear to me:

I'm turning into a grown-up.

I didn't even notice it happening…and I suppose I can't really take much of the credit. It was more of a "process" than an event. It started taking place…oh four or five girlfriends ago.

If there's one lesson I've learned in this life, it's that girls LOVE to fix you.

And that's great because I started out as a mess! Then I started dating one girl (lets protect her identity by calling her *Shmimberly*) and she made me better…too much so as it turns out because I became good enough for this girl *Shmallison* and I dumped Shmimberly. Shmallison made me good enough to break up with her and date her hotter sister, but then her sister helped me get my first good haircut and her best friend had a hot tub so the story continued…

The point is this: Do you plan on staying with your girlfriend?

Yes? Then you might as well let her fix you so she'll stop talking so much during *Sons of Anarchy*.

No? Then you might as well let her fix you so you can get a better one.

FIVE THINGS YOU SHOULD LET YOUR GIRLFRIEND CHANGE

1. Clothes: This is always the first thing they want to change. Your instinct will be to resist because you love your beer league softball t-shirts and jeans that are ripped in an un-trendy "not done by Ed Hardy" kind of way. But you know what? You're a handsome dude. You *should* be dressing better. Let me put it in terms you understand: If you had an autographed Ken Griffey Jr. rookie card, would you store it the ziplock bag that you used for your turkey sandwich yesterday? No. You'd take it to the card shop and get the bolted fiberglass casing and a baller-ass frame so you could hang it above the mantle. Just like Griff deserves a frame, you deserve a pair of Dockers flat-front khakis: the Ken Griffey Jr. autographed rookie card of pants. Also, your girlfriend has a hotter friend and she LOVES a man in Dockers. *Trust me.*

2. Cleaning habits: This one will sneak up on you. These chicks are tricky. If they see you as a "sound investment" then they'll start out by doing some of this for you. They want to get you in the habit of BEING someplace clean before they train you to maintain it. Pretty soon you'll start noticing decorative soap dispensers in your bathroom, clean towels that YOU didn't wash, and neatly paired socks that are in your sock drawer instead of a laundry basket in the living room. Before you know it, you're hooked. Getting into a nicely fixed bed every night is like heroin. Once you do it once, you'll catch the sickness when you forget. I believe that in his book *seven Habits of Highly Effective People*, Stephen Covey points this out. *"These hoes be convincing you that you care about things you never thought about before. I get hives when I know there's a dirty plate in my sink."* My advice? Just go with it. If your house is clean, next time your girlfriend invites her old roommate (Jenni with an "i" who's now a Vikki's Secret model) and her boyfriend Brad over, you'll look like a WAY better option than Brad because he NEVER cleans the mirror in the bathroom...Now it's only a matter of time before you and Jenni with an "i" are taking turns fixing your bed.

3. Drinking habits: Sorry man, you're an adult now. Going out with the fellas and getting hammered four or five nights a week isn't cool. Neither are clubs with names that are missing vowels like PNK or XTRA. The good news is that your girlfriend wants you to slow down anyway. Don't worry, she's got all sorts of other "activities" that you guys can get into (more on that later). The upside is that when you met your girlfriend, her friends were disgusted with how sloshed you were. She was the only one who thought it was "cute" but now that they're seeing you in a more sober light, Katrina and Allison are all "dammmmn he's kinda cute when he's not drooling and sweaty!"

4. Hygiene: It's okay bro, you didn't even know you HAD a hairy back. You can't see it! But she did. So she Nair'ed that shit off for you, and now you look good at the beach. I can tell because her friend who brought out Daddy's boat is checking you out every time you're looking the other way. That might also be because your girlfriend runs every morning and makes you go with her. This is a good thing. "Daddy's Boat" wasn't an option with that beer gut you were working with last summer, but now? Now you may get to check out Daddy's ski cabin this winter after your break up.

5. Activities: Ahh activities. Girlfriends *love* activities. Before her, if I asked you what your weekend plans were, you'd say "I'll probably watch the football games" right? But now they consist of throwing barbecues for the games, going *to* the games, and then making dinner reservations with the Thompsons after the games. You'll be tired after all of your activities, but that's okay because you're not going out to the bars every night, so you'll be in bed by 10pm anyway. Also, all of the girls who ignored you before are now noticing how busy you always are. "Sorry I can't hang this weekend because I've already got plans with Amy" is a hot girl's kryptonite. If there's one thing they hate more than how needy you used to be, it's how unavailable you are to them now.

It all boils down to this: Take your girlfriend's advice. Why? Because it'll make you good enough for a new girlfriend. May the force be with you.

- *Chapter Forty Two* -

I'm Not Arguing...YOU'RE Arguing

This weekend, I got into a huge argument with a girl. It was *brutal*. We were fighting because she wants me to go with her to her sister's wedding. *Apparently* I promised I would go when she asked me...last year...I don't remember promising that, so I was all "you're not the boss of me!"

Then she started crying...dammit. That's our weakness, right guys? Well...that's one of them. It's "crying", "Jean Claude Van Damm movies" and "boobies" but not in that order.

Luckily, it wasn't my first rollercoaster. I've been down this road before. I've been down this road with *her* before. So I just calmly took a deep breath and said:

"You know what? Maybe I *should* come...it would be great to catch up with your mom and listen to her talk about why you're wasting your time with me still. I haven't seen your family in about a year. Am I allowed to laugh when every single one of them asks what I do for a living? Oh wait...There's an open bar right?"

Yeah that's right...Don't you EVER try to manipulate me with tears. I know your tricks better than you do sister...*and* I know how to beat them.

Which leads us to the topic of today's lesson, boys and girls. I hope you're ready for some truth to rain down on you.

Arguing with a women is like going to war...John Rambo said it best in *First Blood 2*, right before he started crying like a little girl:

> **"To win a war you have to become a war"**

What does this mean? I have no clue, he was an abstract dude with lots of layers that I can't begin to comprehend. But my best guess is that it means you pull out all the stops for every argument, no matter how small...that is, if you wanna win....Love is a Battlefield, Baby (Pat Bentar was soo gangster).

10 WAYS TO WIN EVERY ARGUMENT...EVEN WHEN SHE CRIES

1. Deny: Remember that Shaggy song "it wasn't me"? What an inspiration! I mean...aside from doing nasty disgusting things with a random girl on the table we eat off of and then lying to his girlfriend so much she probably had to check into a mental hospital...and not a cool, sexy mental hospital like in *Sucker Punch*; the shitty kind like in *One Flew Over The Cuckoo's Nest*...but that's beside the point: You gotta deny. Women love telling you that you're lying, and you might be, but it doesn't matter. You're the defense attorney at this point and even YOU don't have to believe you. It's about what she can prove. She's looking to trap you on the witness stand and get you to cross your words so she can make up a truth based on your confusion. And no...it's never a good idea to scream "you can't handle the truth!"

2. Fight Fire With Fire: If she's gonna get petty in *every* argument and bring up that time you forgot her birthday (even though you had only been dating a week and she didn't even tell you it was her birthday; she just "assumed you'd pay attention to Facebook" which is ridiculous because I'm selfish and only read things on Facebook that have a direct impact on my life) then it's fair game for you to bring up the fact she's a liar. Every girl is a liar. She pretended to like Anchorman but tells you a year later that she "doesn't get why people say Will Ferrell is so funny", which is just as bad as forgetting her birthday.

3. Make Stuff Up: Make up facts that support whatever your argument is. Fact - women are horrible fact checkers. 97% won't ever check the validity of your argument...even if she has a smart phone (see how easy that is).

4. Avoid hypotheticals: You Can't Win! *Of course* "if she was in a coma and would never find out" you'd sleep with her bff that looks just like Jessica Alba and smells so good you give her extra long hugs every time you run into her...mmmm...wait what was I talking about again? Oh yeah, avoid hypotheticals by changing the subject. **Try this one (it works...believe me):** "I think I saw Kim Kardashian ask her boyfriend the same thing on *Kim and Kourtney take New York*." Even if she doesn't watch the show, it works. For some reason, people get dumber and forget what they're doing when you even *mention* the name Kardashian.

5. Props win arguments: Have you ever gotten so mad you wanna break something of yours? Nope, me neither but I see guys who can't control their emotions all the time. I have to say though...they might be onto something. Breaking one of those stupid prizes you won at a fair can halt any large dispute. **WARNING:** It *has* to be something that shatters into pieces and requires a clean-up. 1.) it'll startle and excite her if you don't over-use this move. And 2.) broads get all 1950s submissive house wife when they have to clean up your anger after a argument (that statement was so sexist that I held my balls while I wrote and typed with one hand...Bang-A-Rang Rufio!)

6. Abandon Logic: Girls learned this trick a long time ago. Logic doesn't win arguments. Logic wins debates. You're not having a debate with the girl who's handcuffed you to a bed frame...You're having an argument. When she snaps at you for coming home at 5pm even though you get off at 4:45 because she "saw a soap opera about a guy who was stopping by his mistresses' house every day on his way home and she had a feeling you were doing the same thing you son of a bitch!" you've gotta be prepared to one-up her. Tell her you had a dream where she was a stripper and kept trying to convince you that she was a ninja instead and started throwing ninja stars at the wall but wouldn't give you a lap dance. WHO YOU GIVING LAP DANCES TO BABY??? BECAUSE IT AIN'T ME!!!

7. Don't ever take sides against the family: If she's pissed off at someone, guess what...so are you. Don't *ever* say "Well I can kind of see his/her point of view." She'll reply "I know it was you...and it breaks my heart," Then she'll kiss you on the cheek before two sweaty Italian guys take you on a ride you won't come back from (women who don't get that reference: stick to dating high school boys...you're broken and useless). But truthfully women just wanna feel like you two are on the same team. For all that's good and holy, give in on this one. There's no "I" in team but there is one in "Internet Porn"

8. Distract: Women have a tendency to feel like they can manipulate any man. And I'm not going to lie, that's because a lot of you are very easily influenced by sex and make decisions based solely on the possibility of losing it. I blame the "American Pie" franchise for this, get some pride you ass clown. But you can play that game too. Next time you're in an argument, tell her she's acting like her mother. She'll forget what you were talking about. Then drop a bomb on her and tell her you've changed your stance on the whole "abortion" issue. It doesn't matter what it was in the first place, this is the **one** political agenda women care about. This is important for two reasons: 1.) it's an easy way to get her to forget why you had glitter all over your forehead last night. And 2.) It's a good reminder of how selfish women can be. Screw healthcare! Forget about the Middle East! My uterus has issues!

9. Ignore her: (I'm not even going to put any support under this one, and you know what? It's going to drive every girl who reads it crazy because they don't have an opportunity to refute what I say)

10. Don't get married: Because if every sitcom ever written is *at all* accurate (and I assume they are, if not I should stop living my life *according to Jim*) then you'll never win an argument again.

- Chapter Forty Three -

Why Do You Hate Fun? What to do When Your Relationship gets too "Relationshippy"

I'm sick of being told I need to grow up. I don't need to grow up, YOU need to grow up.

Girls have been telling me that since I started dating...Which is odd since I was a kid then. Yup...That's right, I've been getting the ladies since kindergarten. Jealous? My early "player" status was probably due to my sweet calf muscles (they developed young). Rebecca Vargas. Kissed her by the barbed wire fence next to the slide. It was hot.

But then I decided I wanted to go play "Butt Ball" and she *lost it*. "You're acting like a child Kevin! How can you be so immature? This relationship is over!"

In retrospect, I may be confusing that lecture with another girlfriend along the way, but the message was the same.

This trend has continued to this day. I swear, if women weren't all soft and pretty and junk, I'd totally go gay.

Side Note: The most immature shit comes out of a woman's mouth when she's yelling at YOU for being a child. She reverts to a ten-year-old. It's really funny. Try it sometime.

Even if I am a child, SO WHAT? Where does it say in the bible that you have to grow up???

John 13:21: And Mary Magdalene Doth Say To Jesus, I TOLD YOU ITS TIME TO STOP PLAYING WIFFLE BALL WHEN THE STREET LIGHTS COME ON! IT'S DINNER TIME AND THEN YOU HAVE MESSIAH STUFF TO DO! THESE LOAVES AREN'T GONNA MULTIPLY THEMSELVES!

I have a job, I pay my bills, I wear sweaters and jackets when it's cold...Hell, I even have a 401k and stock options. Isn't that enough? This ain't a sitcom where the hero has to grow up at the end of 21-minutes. This is real life. I can stay childish as long as I want can't I?

Apparently not. I need to grow up MORE. This *must* be true: Girls who watch "Twilight" say so. Yeah, I play legos. Yeah, I've watched and read all the Harry Potter books. Yeah, I just bought a light saber online. Yeah, I still laugh at fart jokes. Yeah, I play wiffle ball on a regular basis (like Jesus)...And that got me thinking:

Ladies, who the hell are **you** to judge?

You have "juicy" written on the ass of more than one pair of pants. You use every holiday to dress like a prostitute (don't stop this habit or anything, I'm just making a point). You go to happy hour five times a week (because it's not alcoholism if you do it while it's light out). You still use a baby voice when you talk to animals...and most importantly YOU CONTINUE TO DATE GUYS WHO ACT CHILDISH.

Look, I'm not telling you to grow up. That would be hypocritical and boring. But If you go into a relationship with a dude who CLEARLY has a bigger lego collection than you've ever seen, a book shelf full of Harry Potter and garage full of go-karts, waffle ball bats and kick balls? You *probably* shouldn't pick a fight about him being a "child" a few months down the road...because he'll call you a "poop-mouth."

- *Chapter Forty Four* -

The Dating Game: Someone HAS to Lose

I just saw a couple walking down the street hand-in-hand. It was adorable: The woman had her hair in a tight bun, trendy black framed glasses and was wearing a blouse and business skirt. The dude? He was wearing a green t-shirt that read *I fucked fear in the ass!*

"Man...**that** is love," I thought as I walked past. "Clearly these two are willing to accept each other for all their differences and slap society in the face because their love is more important than normal social constructs. This is *Jungle Fever* if Wesley Snipes was white."

(somewhere, Spike Lee just vomited and he has no clue why)

But then I thought about it more and realized that this probably isn't true...Maybe they're just in the "*Do Somethin!*" stage of their relationship. You see, there are several stages that a relationship must go through before it can blossom...before it can turn into something bigger than two people...before it can successfully explode and turn into violent outbursts that entertain/annoy all your friends for weeks to come.

Life isn't a Will Smith movie. Not every relationship is supposed to work out. Sometimes two people are so different that it's meant to end with trips to emergency rooms because she hit you in the head with a picture frame that had some memory that "apparently means nothing to you anymore" and then you can inappropriately reference it in a blog a couple years later...

But back to the point: There are several steps that a bad relationship goes through before it escalates to a break up. It's got stages, just like anything else in life:

- The 3 stages of grief (I hear there are more, but I watch a lot of "24" so I focus on Anger, Revenge and Murdering Terrorists),
- The Alcoholics Anonymous "12 Steps to a miserable life full of complaining"
- And of course, "The Bitch Theory" (you're not ready for this one yet, but stay tuned).

I like to call this process **"We hate each other, but I'm lazy and you don't want to die alone"** ...it's a working title.

Step One: The "According To Jim" Stage

This stage is a simple precursor to the mayhem that will eventually come. This is when you'd rather pay attention to the atrocity that is "According to Jim" (which is somehow on in the background *every time* she decides to tell you about her day and the remote is *always* too far away to reach) than hear her complain about how "Shiela and Debbie at work are planning a birthday party and they keep saying they want double fudge mountain cake when *clearly* neither of them need anything in their lives that have "double" or "fudge" in the title.

Other names for this stage are "Please...just stop talking" and "Yeah that was TOTALLY interesting the first 18 times you told me that"

Step Two: Avoidance

I don't want to talk about this step...damn! Quit sweatin' me.

Step Three: The "Do Somethin!" Stage

This stage is where the "I fucked fear in the ass" t-shirt comes into play. You do everything possible to pick a fight...well, everything short of saying "let's fight". You stop washing your dishes ("You're such a pig"), grow a beard when you know she hates it ("Yeah but then I'm supposed to kiss you?"), play Metallica as loud as you can in the car ("I have a migrane!").

Ladies, you can play too: Smile extra long at waiters ("what the hell was that all about?"), stop offering to split checks ("Okay...I guess I'll pay for this one"), spend too much time with your male coworker ("Who the hell is Keith???")...you know...simple stuff like that.

Other names for this stage are "What do you mean you don't want to go to the Monster Truck Show?" or "Me and Keith ALWAYS laugh about that when we go out for happy hour after work!"

Step Four: The "Okay fine, let's rumble" Stage

This is the stage where you finally do away with all the pretense and say "screw it...we're in a FIGHT". You start the fight with something simple, like saying "I think we're too tough on bullies in this country" and pretty soon she's shouting "You lied about wanting children!" even though you've never even talked about it and you're saying "Yes! I lied! I also think your sister is stupid!" After the first "this isn't working" fight, you can pretty much just start one whenever you want. Politics, religion, dead babies...it's all fair game.

Also known as: "That dress makes you look like a skank" or "What do you mean you think Rick is cute?"

Step Five: Fireworks.

This is exhausting when you're involved in it...but when you're not? It's the sweetest thing ever to watch. There will be a huge fight...then drinking...Then the late night phone call in tears...Then the hook up...Then the fight again in the morning...It gets weird.

Then more late night drinking and tears. Then yelling. Then throwing things. Then keying cars. Then maybe a dog gets kidnapped because "you never really loved that dog anyway and I was ALWAYS the one to feed it and I can't believe you would even fight me on this!" Then there's a few years where a judge orders you not to talk...then you finally move on.

This stage is also known as "Wait...what just happened?"

Do you get the moral of this story??? Basically what I'm trying to tell you is this: The girl who sits two cubicles away from me needs to hurry up and get through these stages so I can stop listening to her bitch about her boyfriend.

- *Chapter Forty Five* -

I Just Feel Like She Doesn't GET Me

I always love girls at first. I love them because they're all pretty and soft and smell good and some of them do this thing with their tongue that's just...magic...anyway. What I'm trying to get at is that this always wears off. I'm a huge nerd. When I find out later that she doesn't like Harry Potter and Star Wars or watch Robot Chicken while playing Legos, I get a little sad. It's always an exact moment of sublime realization too.

I'm sitting there having a conversation and she'll say something like "The Spa was a nice escape. I got to spend some time in quiet just reenergizing and really working on figuring myself out and getting focused and balanced. Just getting my energy together" and I'll be like "just like Luke in the fuckin Degoba System!" and she won't laugh...and I'll just sit there waiting but it never comes. You know what comes instead? A steadily building hatred for everything about her. I'll start looking around and thinking "that pink pillow is stupid" and then it's already over, but I don't go anywhere for a while, I just sit there in bitterness for like 3 weeks, AND THEN I leave and she's always confused and you can't tell a girl you broke up with her because she didn't get your degoba joke, it sounds silly.

So what do you do? You make something up. Which leads us to:

Breaking up

So you know how girls are really stupid? And ladies, before you get all up in arms, I only say that because I think you're faking it...and before you jump on that bandwagon and start saying "Hell yeah! Girl power!" take a second to think about how disrespectful that is. But let me explain:

I broke up with a girl a few weeks back. She took it well, I only have one scar from a picture frame holding a photo of some random stupid event I don't remember that "apparently means nothing to me anymore" and it made me really sit and reflect...wait, sorry I mean SHE made me really sit and reflect. Girls ask you some crazy questions when you break up with them don't they? You mentally prepare to break up with someone for hours. You sit in your car rehearsing before you go in, you spend that whole day running through how she's gonna take it.

Then when you break up with a girl, you enter into arbitration as she tries to convince you why you're wrong...which doesn't make sense to me. If a girl told me she didn't want to be with me, that'd be it. "Okay clearly staying with you would be miserable for me so I'm gonna go...can I have your girl Tiffany's number?" is the only acceptable response in my mind, but I've never been dumped that hard. A girl will change everything about her in this arguing process, and it makes it really hard because every point you make is dismissed. She becomes a fuckin genius (told you I'd tie it all together):

"We don't have the same interests"

"We like ALL the same things! I'm really starting to love every sport, sandwiches and drinking PBR with my buddys after going to the strip club"

"I believe in God and you don't"

"What are you talking about? I love God! I was just afraid of him but you've made me see the light. You helped me find him!"

"You're pro-life and I'm pro-choice"

"What? I LOVE dead babies!"

Okay look...I realize that I titled this section of the book something about "Relationships" (I'm too lazy to look back and see what exactly it was) and it turns out it's all about breaking up with girls or avoiding anything "relationshippy" but a handsome man can't be tied down forever. We gotta be free baby!

- *Chapter Forty Six* -

I Just "Liked" Your Single Status Baby

Every guy has a crazy ex-girlfriend. I don't care if he's a 15-year-old Dungeons & Dragons player with an affinity for poop jokes. He has a crazy ex. Some broad in second grade decided they were dating without telling him, and then when he didn't talk to her on the bus, she called him a "stupid head" every day for three years.

It's a proven fact.

My crazy exes? There have been a few that have left scars...but in all fairness to them, only two or three caused stitches.

One told me that Ghandi would be going to hell because he hasn't accepted Jesus Christ as his personal Lord & Savior. I'm pretty sure she was wearing a halter top that showed off her tramp stamp and a little half-nipple at the time...and we were watching South Park. I'd like to say that was the end of it...but she was really pretty, so I overlooked that for a couple weeks until I went to her cult...I mean church.

The only downside has been that I never got to fully *enjoy* the antics of **your** crazy ex-girlfriends unless I sat there and listened to you complain about how you want her back and blah, blah, blah...And even then, I didn't get to take part in any of the passive-aggressive shenanigans...until now.

Enter Facebook.

I love it when my friends break up on Facebook! I get all the interesting parts of the story, without the boring emotions and feelings. Here are my favorite parts of your break up process:

- Jennifer is now "single" (this is posted 15-seconds after the break up)...Then you get to see 24 guys "like" that status (which is the internet equivalent of buying a girl a drink from across the bar. Man up, bro. Show her your calf muscles! Oh wait, they aren't as sweet as mine? Okay just "like" her status then).
- Jennifer posts something like "Ugggh, I'm SOO over the drama" which is awesome because we all know the real drama is far from over. It's only about to begin as you morph into a crazy ex-girlfriend.
- Dillon posts "It feels good to get out with the boys" and 13 of Jennifer's "friends" comment on that, asking where they're going. *Side Note: Girls LOVE to talk about how close they are with their friends. You share feelings and talk and all sorts of crap that men don't do, but you'd*

NEVER see one of us come up with a devious plot to sleep with a friend's ex.
- Jennifer "Loves going to the gym! It feels sooo good to be back!" because everyone, including the ex, needs to know that she's getting back in "do me" shape. Dillon has a snyde "Good for you babe!" comment on this status. Jennifer deletes it immediately.
- Dillon "has been tagged in Courtney (Jennifer's BFF) Jones album "Kirkland Nights" doing some silly dance.
- Jennifer "Just can't trust ANYONE anymore UGGGGGH!"
- At this point, we get into a phase I like to call "Look at me!" where everything said by either Jennifer or Dillon is a desperate attempt to get each other's attention. "Sometimes you have to cut the dead weight" and "I feel better than I have in years!" should be expected during this period.
- Dillon just bought a house and/or got a promotion and/or is hanging out with his sister because he loves family (pretty much anything that will make Jennifer realize what she's missing).
- Jennifer "is now in a relationship with Scott Smith" (even though Scott Smith has only gone out with Jennifer once).
- Jennifer "is single" again (apparently Scott didn't realize Jennifer was in her "crazy ex" stage until it was too late).
- Jennifer changes relationship status to "I make bad decisions, but I get SUPER excited about them"

Jennifer will go through this process seven more times in the next year of your Facebook friendship with her...And analysts wonder why younger generations are watching less TV. Thank you Zuckerberg.

- Chapter Forty Seven -

Breaking Up is Hard to Do...Here's How to Do It

Look my handsome friends; I've only had my heart broken once.

Sure, there have been other breezies that left me sad, but this was the only one that made me sit around listening to Richard Marx songs while looking at photos of her by the glow of candle light.

Young Kids: photos are what we had before "Facebook Tagging" and the glow of candle light is what we had before the glow of an iphone...Richard Marx was what we had before...um... all the depressing shit you guys listen to.

Even worse, this girl broke up with me *via text message*. We were co-workers. She could have just walked into my office in 15-seconds and done it face-to-face. Granted, then she'd have to watch the flickering overhead florescent light glisten off the flecks of gold in my deep hazel eyes and I was wearing a pair of Dockers Flat Front Khakis and my Burberry tie, so she might have struggled quite a bit…In retrospect, I looked *really* good when I had to dress up for work.

It was painful. No one likes that feeling. You're left wondering "what could I have done differently?" or "How can I get her back" and of course "Why ON EARTH would they remake Rollerball???"

I know ladies…I'm hard to resist when I'm talking about how fragile and vulnerable I was. Every girl wants that sensitive guy, and that's what I am…but you know, in a hard-core hetero way where I shoot M16s from my ATV while hunting California Condors.

Here's what I'm getting at: She went about it all wrong! I've broken up with [*insert reasonable number of girls that doesn't make me sound like a douche*], and I'm still friends with most of them!

So I wanted to give you ALL this guide….not just the handsome men.

Hopefully this will help you the next time you're going to break up with someone. Use this responsibly. Oh and ladies, give me a call when you're done because I hear you're single now.

THE BREAK UP: But not depressing like that Vince Vaughn-Jennifer Anniston flick

1. Don't Get Caught Up In The Details: All you need to say is that you're not happy and you're breaking up. If they ask for specifics, *don't give them any.* People (read: girls) become masterminds when getting dumped. You want no part of this

2. Start a Fight: Sun Tzu's *The Art of War* stresses the element of surprise. This is important in a break up too. Do something that you know will piss your significant other off. It's easy. Trust me, this will start a fight and also, she probably won't mind you breaking up with her. Examples:

- **Girls:** Tell Facebook he's in rehab for his heroin addiction and he could *really* use everyone's prayers because the AIDS treatment is gonna be *sooo* much tougher when you add withdrawals to the mix.
- **Guys:** Next time you're cuddling in bed and she asks "what are you thinking", just be honest with her. Trust me, she won't like it. "I want a sandwich and that blonde chick from the new 90210 covered in maple syrup" isn't a relationship-builder.

3. Do it somewhere fun! Break up with him/her at a mini-golf course or a skating rink. Make a game out of it! "Hey Tony, if you can sink a hole-in-one on the windmill, we can stay together. That way when it ends and you go home, Tony will know it's his fault. Plus, then when you leave, you can get a waffle cone because there are always ice cream shops near mini-golf courses.

4. Use Clichés: I know, I know...everyone tells you not to, but we're pre-conditioned to recognize these as relationship-enders. They'll smooth the road for you to end things. Also, it's gonna be really fun to say "it's not you, it's me" when you know it's her obsession with cats that spurred all this.

5. FELLAS ONLY: Watch *Beaches* or *The Notebook* first. This is important because it will get you used to broads crying and being all sad and stuff. It'll dumb your senses down so when you break up with her and she starts crying, you'll stick to your guns.

6. LADIES ONLY: Watch *The Power of My Vagina*. It'll teach you how powerful you are and how much better off you'll be without him. This will give you the strength you need…okay how many of you Googled that already? Because it's not even a real thing. I totally got you. IDIOTS!

7. Don't Do It With a Text Message: Because who knows…maybe the newspaper industry will collapse so the guy/girl you're dumping will write a book instead and talk about what a shrew you are and how happy he was to run into you last year in your sweat pants and tank-top that had spit up all over it while you walked through Target with your short husband and ugly baby, SARAH.

I hope this helps! Make it easy on them…Then go get some ice cream.

- *Chapter Forty Eight* -

Ex-Games: Which One Will She Be?

My editor's brought it to my attention that throughout this book, I may have unfairly identified several of my ex-girlfriends as "crazy" and that some of them will be "offended" by this.

- A. I'm just kidding. Editors are for people who admit their flawed. I, clearly, am not one of those people.
- B. Fair point ladies...and perhaps I owe you all an apology, but in my defense...I'm not going to give you one.

Why? Because I wasn't lying. You WERE crazy. Not the whole time, but at specific points that may or may not have left me with physical scars and broken windows...and you were definitely crazy after we broke up. I don't blame you for this. It's just science. That's how things happen. I'd be devastated if I'd broken up with me too.

Everyone's ex is "crazy" to some extent or another. I'm pretty sure some of you have described *me* as crazy (although in that case you were wrong. I'm the exception that proves the rule. I'm always awesome).

Question You Are Asking Right Now: So what does a "crazy ex" ever LOOK like Kevin? What are the symptoms? You're a genius, please break it down for us.

Well, I'm glad you asked that. There are several types of crazy exes. Some are good, some are bad, some are both, and some are neither. Confused? Allow me to break it down for you.

PROFILES OF AN EX GIRLFRIEND: Which straw are you going to draw? (answer: the short one)

1. The "Caller" Ex: Do you know what 63 missed calls looks like? I do. It looks like "crazy". And at some point, you get tired of hitting ignore and decide "what's the worst that could happen?" but unfortunately, the worst that could happen is an hour-long conversation about "what she did wrong and what you guys can do better because she's pretty sure you have something special that she's not ready to give up on" while you pray to God almighty that she DOES give up on it and gives up on it quickly so you can get back to the craps table with your friends and start enjoying life again because you have a year-and-a-half to recover from.

2. The "Friends with Benefits" Ex: These ones are good at masking their "crazy". Adding the benefits was their idea. They like to tell you "oh no we're just having fun" but they're not just having fun. Women can't do that. They have all these "feelings" and "emotions" that get in the way of fun. Before you know it, that "fun" will turn into "why aren't we still together?" conversations and "oh so I'm good enough to fool around with but not good enough to date?" And then BAM! You're back in a relationship, but this time with a healthy dose of "guilt" at the core. I call this a "Catholic" relationship.

3. The "Hater" Ex: Personally, I'm super charming when I break up with a girl and I look great in my Dockers Flat-front khakis as I walk away. That tends to disarm them, so I've never experienced the hater. But from what I hear, this is a typical crazy ex. She'll blow up at you when you do the dumping, and then call to remind you that she hates you. Chances are you'll hear from other people around town that you cheated on her and/or she was cheating on you. It doesn't matter. Let her be angry now because if she doesn't get it out, she'll develop a vindictive, insecure complex that inspires her to "accidentally" get pregnant while dating her next boyfriend. Trust me...I've seen this in movies and you OWE it to mankind to not let this one reproduce.

4. The "Stalker" Ex: Every guy wants to pretend he's got a stalker ex, but the truth is that they're harder to come by than you'd think. Marky Mark in *Fear* is a stalker ex. *Jade* is a stalker ex. My buddy Tim's girl who would show up at ever bar we'd go to and just sit on the other side of the room staring at him with a piercing hatred that suggested a capability for murder and then be waiting for him in the driveway when we got home...that's a stalker ex. Your girlfriend who knows what Facebook pictures you've been tagged in since you broke up? Not a stalker ex.

5. The "Make You Jealous" Ex: Ahh the ex who wants to prove she was too good for you. She goes out and dates everyone you know, buys them things that she then posts pictures of on Facebook, and basically tries to prove "what a good girlfriend she would have been if you hadn't been such an idiot". **Side Note:** *If you find yourself dating a girl who spends a lot of time and energy on you, thank her ex-boyfriend. He's the reason her insecurities just bought you an X-Box.*

6. The "Consistent Date" Ex: This is one of those good cases. You still hang out, play wingman for each other at weddings and do all the stuff you were in such a comfort-zone about when you were dating, but none of the "benefits" and by "benefits" I mean "naked stuff". It's not a bad situation either because you both pretend to be okay with the other person dating, so she won't hassle you about girls you meet...but only until one of you finds someone new, then you'd better prep for the night she has thirteen appletinis and calls you to say she thinks you guys should give it another shot.

7. The "Perfect Storm" Ex: She freaked out, started dating a Marine and moved away as soon as you guys broke up, so now all of her hot friends hate her and love hanging out with you...Maybe this one is too specific for most of you to relate to, but I don't care; a big shout out to all of Kim's hot friends! Lets party this weekend!

8. The "See I fixed myself!" Ex: You broke up and she IMMEDIATELY hit the gym and a diet. She's gotta prove to you that she's better than you deserve, but she's not a whore like No. 5. You won't hear from her for about 6 months, but once you do? She's going to look GREAT, have a sweet new job, and seem emotionally stable...the only problem? She's just realizing that she's too good to make the same old mistakes with you, but tell her to give me a call. She's not too good for a brand new mistake.

Now that you've broken up with her, feel free to start all over with a new girl. That's the best part of being a handsome man! And THAT is how you win at a relationship.

Epilogue: A Handsome Man Would Have Learned Something

Now that you've learned everything you can about being handsome, are you ready to go out into the world?

Trick question, there's no way to learn everything you can about being a handsome man. We're complex creatures with many different levels to us. It would take years to learn everything.

Luckily for you, this book will be wildly successful and I'll be allowed to write sequels, but for now, let me outline the key takeaways from THIS book:

...you know what? I just wrote 224 pages and I'm tired, so fuck it. You get the idea. Stay sexy my friends.

- Love, Kevin

Printed in Great Britain
by Amazon.co.uk, Ltd.,
Marston Gate.